ROMANIA

A Developing Socialist State

WESTVIEW PROFILES
NATIONS OF CONTEMPORARY
EASTERN EUROPE

† Available in hardcover and paperback.

ROMANIA
A Developing Socialist State

Lawrence S. Graham

Westview Press / Boulder, Colorado

Nations of Contemporary Eastern Europe

Copyright © 1982 by Westview Press, Inc.

Published in 1982 in the United States of America by
    Westview Press, Inc.
    5500 Central Avenue
    Boulder, Colorado 80301
    Frederick A. Praeger, Publisher

Library of Congress Cataloging in Publication Data
Graham, Lawrence S.
  Romania, a developing socialist state.
  (Nations of contemporary Eastern Europe)
  Bibliography: p.
  Includes index.
  1. Romania—Politics and government—20th century. I. Title. II. Series.
DR267.G7   320.9498   81-16493
ISBN 0-89158-925-2   AACR2

Printed and bound in the United States of America

089211

For Nicolae and Daniela

Two Romanians unknown to each other
who in their own special ways
opened up so much of their country for me and my family

Contents

Photographs

Preface

This book is intentionally an orthodox and yet unorthodox treatment of Romania. It is orthodox in the sense that it seeks to cover those topics basic to any introductory discussion of a country's government and politics – a description of the country's setting, historical background, basic governmental structure, current political dynamics, and domestic and foreign policy considerations. It is unorthodox in its emphasis on Romania's status as a middle-range developing socialist state in the broader European context and in its fusion of the perspectives offered by political science and public administration.

In focusing on Romania's status as a developing nation it utilizes the concepts and perceptions of development politics and administration in a European setting. Far too often postwar Romania is presented to the outside world as simply another variant of Eastern European politics. From this perspective the fundamental dividing line is the ideological division between Eastern and Western Europe. My approach emphasizes Romania's status as a bridge country, not only in its East-West axis (which is ideological and cultural) but in its North-South axis (which is economic and historical) as well. The former reflects the well-known consequences of Great Power politics and outcomes of World War II; the latter, a fascinating mix of internal and external societal dynamics that calls attention to the contrast between industrial and industrializing societies in Europe as a whole.

In European politics, economics, and society, those countries that early underwent the Industrial Revolution are sharply divided from those that are comparative latecomers to the process of building an industrial economy and a commercialized agriculture. Most discussions of Western European politics deal with this division in historical and cultural terms, as though there were an unstated, inherent difference between North and South. In this context, especially in introductory comparative politics texts that treat only the major European states, Italy almost always appears as the deviant case–a society of conflict that today is an integral part of the European Economic Community, yet whose Mediterranean south continues to lag behind the industrial north.

In the larger European setting–one that emphasizes the necessity of beginning first with the European cultural region as a whole before proceeding with the analysis of any of its economic and/or cultural subregions (be they northern, central, or southern; eastern or western; Nordic or Latin)–Romania constitutes one of the most-different cases. In theoretical discussions of comparative politics, much has been written on the pros and cons of utilizing the most-similar as opposed to the most-different cases in comparative work. A premise behind this study is that there is much to be gained in wider comparative analysis at this point by taking the most-different-case approach in European politics. Given the extensive studies available on the United Kingdom, France, Germany, and Italy, much more work needs to be devoted to the smaller, less well-known, less developed countries. My own fieldwork in Europe began in the early 1970s with one such case in the southwestern part of the Continent–Portugal–and has proceeded to the southeast.

In a real sense Romania is a bridge. Situated in the Balkans, an area long subjected to invasions by various peoples and characterized by great cultural diversity, this country faces both East and West.

One way to gain insight into the collective psychology of the Romanian people is to begin with their language. Approximately 80 percent of spoken Romanian contains words of Latin derivation.[1] Yet modern Romanian, although a Romance language, is substantially different from Italian, French, Portuguese, and Spanish. The only instance where the vulgar Latin of the Eastern empire has evolved into a modern language synonymous with a nation-state, Romanian alone in this language group has kept the case forms. To this base must be added the influence of languages and cultures belonging to other peoples in southeastern Europe with whom Romanians have interacted over the centuries, most notably those of Slavic origin. Not only is there a high incidence of Slavic vocabulary in modern Romanian, but it is also an inflected language in which the common articles have become suffixes, not prefixes as in other neo-Latin tongues.

Although Romanian nationalism has been identified since the nineteenth century with the assertion of the country's Latinity, Slavonic influences are an equally important part of the country's cultural heritage. The most notable example of the latter is found in the rich cultural heritage provided by Romanian Orthodoxy—the church's liturgy, writings, and pictographs were expressed in Cyrillic until well into the nineteenth century. Another dimension of this cultural influence is encountered in what are today Romanian-speaking areas of the Soviet Union, most notably the Moldavian Soviet Socialist Republic, where the Russian state as a part of official policy has dictated that modern Moldavian is not only a language distinct from that spoken in the neighboring Socialist Republic of Romania but an inseparable part of Slavic culture, with a Cyrillic alphabet.

As a way of introducing the student and the general reader to modern Romania, this study utilizes five basic topics or modules that I consider crucial for understanding Romanian government and politics. First examined is the historic role played by nationalism—how it gave rise to the formation of an independent state during the latter part of the nineteenth century and the circumstances leading to the creation of a Greater Romania before World War II. From an image of society and politics at the time of Romania's maximum territorial extension, the second chapter moves into an analysis of the forces that destroyed Old Romania: fascism and communism. For those currently in power, the change in the spelling of the country in the mid-1960s from Rumania (or "Roumania" in British usage) to Romania symbolizes a great deal: a reaffirmation of the country's distinct national heritage and an attempt to indicate that the new society was radically different from the old.

In Chapter 3, attention shifts to a discussion of the evolution that the country has experienced under socialism and how and why there has been a rekindling of nationalism since the mid-1960s. Once the character of the present-day Romanian Communist party as a mass organization and the fusion of party and state organs have been established, the book focuses on the theme of socioeconomic development, both as a set of policies and as a series of programs. Finally, Romania's position in the modern world as a middle-range developing socialist state is assessed by examining its position in Europe, where it is a Soviet dependency, as well as its cultivation of friendly relations with nonaligned Third World countries.

Inherent in this approach is an attempt to approximate Romanian reality through a more complete understanding of the state than is contained in most contemporary political science literature. Political science in the United States is identified with a perspective whereby far too often all aspects of contemporary governments are subsumed under the category of the political. This book departs from that tradition by incorporating the vantage point offered by public administration. Although the political is an undeniable aspect of that which is "public," large-scale, complex organizations – that is to say, state bureaucracy or state administration – frequently take on a life of their own. From my perspective, comparative politics in general and studies of Eastern Europe in particular have not devoted adequate attention to the bureaucratic determinants of political behavior. This approach, then, is one that emphasizes not only the significance of language and culture as a way of gaining insight into politics but also the importance of developing an integral view of the governmental process by considering public organizations to be of such complexity and importance in the modern state as to require separate analysis.

NOTES

1. In a word count of Latin-based words in modern Romanian Alexandru Rosetti, a leading Romanian philologist, reported the following findings: a total of around 6,700 words of Latin origin, of which 1,000 to 1,500 constitute basic vocabulary in Romanian. Of the basic words used most frequently 60 percent are of Latin origin and 20 percent are of Slavic origin. In this study Rosetti also reported that of the 3,607 words analyzed by Mihai Eminescu prior to World War II, 46.6 percent were of Latin origin with a frequency of 83 percent, while 18.81 percent were of Slavic origin with a frequency of 6.93 percent. Rosetti's work can be compared with that of Carlo Tagliavini's broader study of the Romance languages. According to Tagliavini, in the only complete etymological dictionary of Romanian (1870-1879), of the 5,765 words studied, Latin influence is much less – 1,165 words of Latin origin and 4,600 of foreign origin (2,361 Slavic, 965 Turkish, 635 Neo-Hellenic, 589 Hungarian, and 50 Albanian). Recognizing the imprecise nature of these figures, for purposes here the important statistic is the one referring to spoken Romanian – Eminescu's frequency count of the most commonly used words, which runs at 83 percent. As is true of other languages, but more so in Romanian – given the importance of the oral tradition as a way of maintaining a core Romanian culture – one must be ready to distinguish between erudite Romanian and popular forms of the language. Slavic words increase in written, formally expressed Romanian. But most Romanian philologists are quick to stress in basic language courses that the use of Latin-based vocabulary is the most rapid way to develop an ability to communicate.

Romanian has four principal dialects. The major one is classified as Daco-Romanian – the language spoken in Romania today as well as in Bessarabia, in that part of Bucovina annexed by the USSR after World War II, in the section of the Banat that belongs to Yugoslavia, and in some villages in Bulgaria and Hungary near the present Romanian border. The other dialects have no relationship to nation-state formation and are of declining importance, although Macedonian – Romanian (*Macedorumeno*), of which there are some 150,000 speakers in

Albania, recalls the presence of a historical residue of spoken Latin throughout the Balkans. See Alexandru Rosetti, *Schiță de istorie a limbii române de la origini și pînă în zilele noastre* [A sketch of the history of the Romanian language from its origins down to our times] (București: Editura Albatros, 1976), p. 14; and Carlo Tagliavini, *Le origin delle lingue neolatine: introduzione alla filologia romanza* [The origin of the neo-Latin languages: an introduction to romance philology] (Bologna: Casa Editrice Prof. Ricardo Patròn, 1959), pp. 268, 301–305.

Acknowledgments

For their kindness and help in showing us what life in Romania is like for its citizens, I want to thank the many Romanians we came to know during our year in their country. They come from all walks of life: university professors, hotel personnel, school teachers, students, clergy in the Romanian Orthodox church, researchers, party officials, peasants, workers, gypsies, and bureaucrats. Equally important are a number of U.S. nationals: Gerson Sher (now at the National Science Foundation) and his successors in the Section on the USSR and Eastern Europe of the National Academy of Sciences (NAS); George Hoffman and Edward Taborsky, colleagues at the University of Texas (Austin); and Earl A. Pope, professor of religion at Lafayette College, companion during my year in Romania and source of the photographs printed here.

For the opportunity to conduct fieldwork in Romania, I am indebted to NAS's National Research Council, the Romanian Academy, and Professor Ioan Matei of the Sociological Institute, through whom my program was arranged. I alone take responsibility for the viewpoint expressed in this study.

L.S.G.

Political Map of Contemporary Romania

Source: Adapted from maps provided by the Geographic Institute (Bucharest).

1

Nationalism and the Formation of an Independent Romanian State

Since the late 1960s, Romania—a medium-size southeastern European state, large by Balkan standards but slightly smaller than the U.S. state of Oregon—has attempted to present an image to the outside world different from that of its neighbors. Romania has emphasized that it is a country apart from the rest of the Eastern bloc. Although its party leadership has never gone to the extreme followed by Tito in Yugoslavia—nor has it ever really had that option—both Gheorghe Gheorghiu-Dej and Nicolae Ceauşescu have striven to maximize national autonomy without triggering a break with Moscow and thereby inviting direct Soviet intervention such as that which occurred in Hungary and Czechoslovakia.

The symbol of this negotiated autonomy has been an independent foreign policy based on the principle of good relations with all peoples and the conscious pursuit of concrete ties with the Western countries. The means whereby this has been achieved has been cultivation of close relations with the People's Republic of China and continuation into the 1980s of the Sino-Soviet split within the socialist camp. But, how independent is Romania really? Or, conversely, how dependent is Romania on the Soviet Union? Another way to state the question is to raise an old issue in the development of modern Romania: Does Romania essentially face East and hence must it remain closely integrated with Russian political, social, and cultural developments? Or, does it face West and constitute an integral part of Western experience? No Romanian would deny the reality of Russian hegemony in this area of the world and the implications of an extended common frontier with the Soviet Union. Yet, no less today do Romanian leaders want the country to become a full participant in European development than was the case over a century ago when, in carving out a state that would coincide with the nation, that generation of leaders confronted a declining but still very

1

real Turkish hegemony to the east and an Austro-Hungarian one to the west.

To answer these questions it is necessary first to establish a brief profile of contemporary Romania. Romania currently has a population in the neighborhood of 21.6 million (21,559,416, according to the most recent available figures). For a country that was previously a rural society–an underdeveloped agrarian state–notable transformations have taken place over the past thirty years. These changes are reflected in the fact that today 43 percent of the population can be classified as urban and the remaining 57 percent rural, where it is concentrated in small villages (sate). Fifteen cities in Romania have a population of over 100,000 each; of these, five–Cluj, Iaşi, Braşov, Galaţi, and Timişoara–exceed 200,000. But, as is true of so many countries with histories of governmental and economic centralism, one city–Bucharest, the nation's capital, with a population of 1.7 million–far exceeds all others in size. It is here that the country's most important decisions have always been made and where the major economic, technical, and human resources are located.

SPATIAL DIMENSIONS AND CONSIDERATIONS

More so than any other part of the Balkans, the physical area occupied by Romania today (237,500 square kilometers–91,699 square miles) has long served as a crossroads, east and west, north and south. As can be seen by examining Map 1, to the east and the north one encounters the Soviet Union, specifically the Ukraine and the Moldavian SSR. This proximity to the Soviet Union–physical, economic through trade, and cultural (for centuries Kiev was a major center of cultural diffusion)–is an inescapable fact in Romanian life. Other Slavic culture areas are to be found to the south in Bulgaria, whose close linguistic, cultural, and economic ties with the Soviet Union are a well-known fact, and to the southwest in Yugoslavia. Separating Bulgaria from the Soviet Union is 150 miles (242 kilometers) of Romanian Black Sea coastline. The outstanding features of this brief bit of coast are the seaport of Constanţa, with its beach resort areas to the north and the south, and the Danube Delta (Tulcea), where vast expanses of marshland constitute a rich and varied wildlife preserve. At the old mouth of the delta, today a portion of enclosed sandy coast, is the archaelogical site of Istria, an ancient Greco-Roman Black Sea port of much interest. This geographic setting makes it easy to appreciate the image often evoked by Romanians of their country as a Latin island in the midst of a Slavic sea.

Directly to the west is Hungary, a country that while not Slavic constitutes an equally important source of cultural conflict. For a thousand years – from the Hungarian point of view – what is today the western third of Romania, the region called Transylvania, was considered an integral part of Hungary. But since the end of World War I the language spoken by the majority of the population has been the determining criterion, and the area has been defined as Romanian in accord with the region's dominant nationality. But there has always been and continues to be an important Magyar-speaking minority in Transylvania, today estimated at 9 percent of the population. In certain zones Magyar speakers actually constitute a majority of the population and for all of them the old Austro-Hungarian city of Cluj remains their cultural center.

National Minorities

Mention of the common frontier with Hungary on the west and the continued presence of a vocal Hungarian or Magyar/Szekler minority introduces another important element in developing a profile of contemporary Romania. Despite the definition of Romania as state and nation in ethnic and linguistic terms that set it apart from its neighbors, there are important minority groups within the country for whom these symbols of nationality have no meaning. Furthermore, not all areas where the Romanian-speaking population is dominant are currently synonymous with national frontiers. In this regard Romania is very much part of Central Europe. This is a region where borders have remained fluid and where sizable national minorities have plagued each of the national governments from the time of their first formation. After all, it was the nationalities question that brought about the demise of the Austro-Hungarian Empire and that continues to trouble relations with the Soviet Union.

Second in size to the Hungarian minority is Romania's Germanic population. It is currently estimated at 2 percent, but is of declining importance. Saxons and Swabians have lived in western Romania since medieval times and have left an indelible mark on towns such as Sibiu, Braşov, and Hunedoara. They are also a highly valued minority because they include a high proportion of the most economically productive sectors of the population. For the most part, though, the Germanic population no longer feels strong ties to Transylvania and many have emigrated to the Federal Republic of Germany since the 1950s.

Although the Romanian government has been reluctant to see its German population leave, it has been quite willing to facilitate the emigration of the country's third most important minority group – the Jews. Prewar Romania had one of the largest concentrations of Jews in Central Europe, if not the largest. But today that population, which once numbered close to 750,000 and was concentrated in urban areas and in commerce and trade east of the Carpathians, numbers between 40,000 and 50,000. However one should be quick to note that this reduction in Romania's Jewish minority is not a consequence of extermination campaigns identified with Hitler's Third Reich, but rather is the result of an open policy of permitting Romanian Jews to emigrate to Israel. Romania alone of the Eastern European states has cultivated good relations with contemporary Israel and has maintained diplomatic ties consistently throughout the postwar years. The exit of this minority has removed an element that was important in Old Romania, especially in such areas as Iaşi (city as well as district), where preindustrial urban life was closely identified with a Jewish-Romanian subculture. Although few if any nationals will speak of the issue today, there were those in Iaşi as elsewhere in Central Europe who lost their lives in the war years because of their faith and as a consequence of fascism, the Romanian variant of which was known as the Iron Guard (or, more formally, the Legion of the Archangel Michael).

A final group that warrants mention and that is set aside from the 85 percent of the population usually defined as ethnic Romanians is the gypsy population, the *romani* who have always constituted an integral part of the mix that has emerged as modern Romania. The problem here is that since this group does not exist officially it is difficult to estimate its size and importance. All that can be said, consequently, is that there is a *romani* minority that is obvious to anyone who has spent an extended time in the country. The gypsy population is found either in distinctive mobile communities or assimilated as families and individuals into the mainstream of contemporary Romanian life.

Religion as Culture

No discussion of the formation of Romania as a nation-state would be complete without inclusion of the Romanian Orthodox church. For centuries, especially in Transylvania, identification with Eastern Orthodoxy has constituted an integral part of establishing one's "Romanianness." Faith, when combined with language spoken and family name, has long served as a basis for determining ethnicity. Even today, in a regime that is officially Marxist-Leninist and hence atheistic, the church continues to play a vital role and one frequently encounters a tolerance of Romanian Orthodox church activities as a device for reinforcing identity with Romanian culture. While other religious groups—Roman Catholic, Protestant, Jewish, Islamic, and various other branches of the Orthodox church—are tolerated and regulated through a bureaucratic entity known as the Department of Cults, formed prior to the transition to socialism, none has benefited to the extent of Romanian Orthodoxy. This can be seen in the maintenance of church buildings being considered a valuable portion of the country's cultural heritage (many are still used for religious services and inhabited by religious orders), state contributions to priests' salaries, and the sanctioning of such income-producing activities as the sale of candles and icons.

Regional Differences

Despite these integrating influences – the emphasis on Romanian nationality in the context of a nation-state with a declining minority population – Romania retains marked internal differences. The basic dividing line cutting across the country continues to be the Carpathian Mountains, forming a "U" or a curve facing West. East of the Carpathians is what is frequently referred to as the "Old Kingdom," containing the United Principalities of Moldavia (to the north) and Wallachia (on the Danubian plains to the south). This is the part of Romania that historically has had the longest experience with self-rule, although not necessarily consecutive regimes. Early in the nineteenth century, with Russian support, these two principalities established considerable autonomy under Turkish rule. With the growth of nationalism and its focus on creating a single independent state for all Romanians, the union of Moldavia and Wallachia took place in 1859, largely through the leadership provided by Alexandru Ioan Cuza. In 1878, when political independence became official, and in 1881, when this new state was declared a kingdom (regat), Romania emerged on the map as a distinct entity under a constitutional monarchy closely modeled after French political institutions, with Bucharest as the nation's capital.

In 1918, with the breaking up of the Austro-Hungarian Empire, the area west of the Carpathians – Transylvania – was joined to Romania on the grounds that the majority of its population was Romanian in language and culture. These "new territories" were then and remain substantially different from the rest of the country. Centuries of Hungarian rule over the region – whether for good (the Hungarian perspective) or for bad (the Romanian viewpoint) – has given this area of the country a distinctly Western character. Here for example the first printing of the Romanian language took place utilizing a Latin alphabet rather than Cyrillic. Such cities as Braşov, Sibiu, and Cluj became important not only commercially and governmentally but also culturally, serving as centers for diffusing European values and norms. Religious pluralism has also been far more common in these areas. Complementing Eastern Orthodoxy, emphasized as the religion of the Romanian population in Transylvania, are Roman Catholicism (historically the state religion of Hungary and the faith of the Magyars), the Uniate churches (formed by Romanians who kept the Orthodox liturgy but acknowledged the authority of Rome rather than that of the Romanian or the Ecumenical Patriarchs), the older Protestant churches (Lutheran,

Reformed, and Unitarian, identified largely with the German- and Hungarian-speaking population), and the newer Protestant groups (Baptist, Seventh Day Adventist, Pentecostalist, and Evangelical Brethren). No less important has been the greater economic prosperity of the region in both rural and urban areas. It has long been recognized by Romanians that the quality of life west of the Carpathians is much better than that to the east.

Today, despite substantial and real economic growth throughout Romania, these economic and cultural differences remain significant. Some explain them in terms of extended Turkish rule over Moldavia and Wallachia, in which contact with the West was cut off for centuries and industrialization nonexistent. Others call attention to the impoverished quality of the land in much of this area, especially that around Iași, and the limited prospects for industrialization in terms of raw materials and markets. Yet one should be quick to add that not only is Bucharest the most important industrial center in the country but Ploiești, to the north in the heart of what were originally productive oil fields, is the center of Romania's petrochemical industry and Pitești, adjacent to coal-producing areas and northeast of Bucharest, is a booming industrial area focused around steel production. Likewise, the Danubian plains are the seat of a rich agricultural area, especially grains, and important wine-producing areas extend to the east and north. All these areas are to be found east of the Carpathians.

Besides the distinctive character of Moldavia, Wallachia, and Transylvania, the Banat to the southwest (with the city of Timișoara), Bucovina in the northeast, and Dobruja (the Black Sea coast area south of Constanța) are equally varied regions. One could go considerably farther by calling attention to other subcultural regions. For example, the agricultural communities and small towns along the backbone of the Carpathians are markedly different from the villages and small commercial centers of the plains areas. Each of these regions is also distinctive in its popular art – especially embroidery, peasant dress, and music – all of which give expression to internal differences.

Romanians Outside Romania

Last, in establishing an initial profile of modern Romania, one should realize that not all areas where the Romanian population is in the majority today are synonymous with the boundaries of this nation-state. At the time of Romania's maximum extension between the two world wars, both northern Bucovina (the region just north of Suceava) and Bessarabia (the region between the Prut River, Romania's current border with the Soviet Union on the east, and the Dnester River) formed parts of Greater Romania. The incorporation of Bessarabia into the Moldavian

SSR is a particularly sensitive issue, as much of this area was identified historically with the Principality of Moldavia and was long considered a core part of a well-defined Romanian-speaking area whose existence as a cultural region stretched back across the centuries.

Herein lies one of the principal problems of modern Romania: how to reconcile concepts of nationality and community that historically have been fluid in terms of geographic space with the current reality of a world of nation-states in which fixed borders set the limits of the state. In this regard Romania remains today as in the past a fragile state, one whose borders and limits could easily become the subject of redefinition should the international distribution of power in this area of the world undergo redefinition. For the present Romanian leaders are quite willing to consider the question of Bessarabia closed so long as the issue of Romanian sovereignty over Transylvania, as a whole or in zones, is not raised.

NATION AND STATE BUILDING

With spatial considerations – the physical location of present-day Romania and its current frontiers – in mind, the dynamics of Romanian nationalism and its expression in the form of nation-state building over the last century can be discussed. In Romania, as in other states in southern Europe, nation-state building goes hand in hand with the desire to modernize – with the desire to create the conditions necessary for sustained socioeconomic progress and for raising the standard of living to approximate that of northwestern Europe. To understand this set of national experiences requires that one abandon for the time being the perspective that the basic division in the European region is that between Western and Eastern Europe.

The Integrity of Southern Europe

A useful way to conceptualize the broad thrust in Romanian development – the focus on nation-state building and sustained socioeconomic progress that has preoccupied Romanian government leaders for the last century – is to utilize the viewpoint developed by a group of French historians known as the Annales School (the particular group of scholars who have published much of their work in the *Annales: economies, societés, civilisation*) and especially by Fernand Braudel. To this perspective should be added the preoccupation of an earlier generation of Spanish scholars who flourished during the years of the Republic – the Generation of 1898 – and some of the essays and ideas of José Ortega y Gassett. While there is much that separates these writers, they share a view that emphasizes the importance of considering the development of modern Europe in terms of two distinct patterns of evolution and development. For them, northern Europe is primarily oriented toward the North Atlantic and has been and is the center of highly developed industrial economies. In contrast, southern or Mediterranean Europe is a much older area, culturally speaking, which was until modern times the center of political conflict and change where three great civilizations converged: Greco-Latin, which influenced the formation of Western culture and flourished in southwestern Europe during the fourteenth, fifteenth, and sixteenth centuries; Islamic, as expressed in the institutions and culture of the Ottoman Turks; and Byzantine, which has survived into modern times only in religious terms, as a part of the cultural heritage identified with the Orthodox churches of the eastern Mediterranean. From Braudel's perspective this cultural difference is inseparable from geographic and spatial considerations. From that of the traveler, regardless of the country examined, the milieu of southern Europe – be it southeastern or southwestern – gives expression to a very different reality than that of northern Europe.

While Braudel emphasizes the integrity of the Mediterranean region as a whole, for the purposes of discussing Romania reference to southern Europe alone is appropriate – the area extending from the Iberian peninsula on the west, across the Italian peninsula, to the Balkan peninsula on the east. All the states in this subregion are latecomers to the Industrial Revolution and, regardless of the levels of culture and development achieved in times past, all are similar in that despite great socioeconomic progress over the last fifty years, each remains in one way or another a dual economy – one sector advanced and modern in terms of current European norms; the other, underdeveloped and traditional, yet richly varied in the peasant and small-town subcultures that have survived.

Consider the extremes of the southern European area for a moment: Portugal and Romania. They are dissimilar in many ways. Not only was Portugal Europe's first nation-state, it is presently an underdeveloped mixed-economy country dependent on the United States and the major western European states. Romania, on the other hand, is comparatively a more advanced middle-range developing socialist economy dependent on the Soviet Union. Yet, from the standpoint of comparative linguistics, Carlo Tagliavini has called attention to similarities in language that bind together what were peripheral areas of the Roman world and modern Europe as well – Romanian, Continental Portuguese, and Sicilian. Economically and politically Romania and Portugal are both dependent nations that have had to live for a long time with the reality that their options in terms of national development have been constrained by the Great Powers that surround them.

Within this framework Romania stands at the outer limits. Depending on which area of the country one cares to focus upon, one can make a case for its inclusion in a Slavic culture area by concentrating on Moldavia (northeastern Romania and the Moldavian Soviet Socialist Republic); in central Europe – along with Hungary and Czechoslovakia – by calling attention to Transylvania and the new nation that has emerged since the 1950s, first as a "people's republic" and later as a "socialist republic"; or in southern Europe by considering the Danubian plains and their extension eastward to the Black Sea (Wallachia, with its distinctive subregions, Oltenia and Muntenia).

The Concept of Latinity

None of this would warrant such detailed discussion were it not for the fact that the current leadership, like that before World War II, defines Romanian nationality in terms of the nation's Daco-Roman past. A large part of this cult of Romania's Roman heritage is derived from the dispute with Hungary over who has a right to Transylvania. The Hungarian thesis argues for an earlier Magyar presence and the later migration of Romanian-speaking peoples into this region. The Romanian side emphasizes the presence of a core Daco-Romanian culture dating back to antiquity. It stresses the continuity between past and present: the acculturation of the Dacians to Roman civilization and language (although Dacia was a part of the Roman Empire for less than a century); the fact that the vulgar Latin spoken by these people provides an unbroken linguistic tie across the centuries; and the way they survived countless invasions in the region by taking refuge in the Carpathian mountains, returning to the plains on both sides in times of peace. In support of this thesis, the state has made available over the years extensive resources for archaeological work, especially in Transylvania. A good example of this use of historical and archaeological materials to support the thesis of continuous occupation of these areas is to be found in the small but well-developed museum of history in Cluj.

There is no reason here to enter into the details and evidence used to support the Romanian thesis. What is instructive is the long existence of a sense of community among these people – expressed in language, religion, and a popular culture that predates the formation of the modern Romanian state. As is true elsewhere in the Balkans (most notably in contemporary Greece), the concept of nationality and the desire to bring together all those sharing a common tongue and culture emerged well in advance of the formation of an independent nation-state. When it did become possible in the nineteenth century to give concrete expression to these very old aspirations for sustained self-rule, the modernizing elite looked westward, especially to France, for an appropriate model.

Although the establishment of autonomy for Moldavia and Wallachia was due primarily to the support of tsarist Russia, once union took place and the drive to modernize the country got underway, the new leadership embarked on a campaign not only to remove all traces of Turkish rule from national life but also to downplay Slavic influence. In this context the distinctive binding force behind Romanian nationalism was an appeal to the past, predating the centuries of Turkish rule and reaffirming the country's Latin heritage. Combined with this interest in historical self-discovery was a conscious attempt to reshape the language by rooting out Slavic influences and incorporating a neo-Latin vocabulary. This was especially the case where the coming of new technology and skills introduced concepts for which there was no adequate expression in Old Romanian. The language to which they turned was French. French influence in late-nineteenth-century Romania extended far beyond language; it was reflected in dress, in architecture (especially in the design of streets, buildings, and parks for Bucharest), in the arts – literature, painting, and music. This francophone orientation of the "liberal" elite was linked to their desire to overcome the legacy of centuries of Turkish rule, with its suppression of Romanian culture, by Westernizing the country as rapidly as possible. But they were "liberals" only in the sense that, as compared with pro-Russian "conservative" landowners and those aristocrats who looked eastward, they wished to build a new Romania clearly aligned with the West. In their minds progress, change, and Westernization were synonymous.

In a society where the gap between the rulers and the ruled was already enormous, this first wave of modernization served to heighten, not reduce, class differences. Rural Romania, where the majority of the population lived, remained largely untouched by these changes. There a lively peasant society centered in small villages, with distinctive dress and a rich oral tradition, continued unabated while the new elite – landowners, merchants, professional politicians, intellectuals – cultivated a life style and outlook emphasizing all that was European. The arts drew upon popular culture to some extent, but they too took the form prescribed by European norms of the day.

National Autonomy

In this initial period of nation-state building, six dates stand out as convenient benchmarks for the general reader. The events of 1848–1849 are significant not only because they signal the first concrete expression of the desire to unify all Romanian-speaking people on both sides of the Carpathians into a single state, but also because they call attention to changes taking place in southeastern Europe as a whole. These years mark a series of revolts upsetting existing relations throughout the

Austro-Hungarian and Ottoman empires. It was this larger context that created an appropriate environment for establishing the autonomy of Wallachia and Moldavia and for awakening a consciousness of national identity among the Romanian-speaking majority in Transylvania. Then, as now, the shape given to Romania was determined more by external circumstance than internal pressures for change.

In 1859 the formal act of unification of Moldavia and Wallachia took place. In 1866 Carol of Hohenzollern became ruler of the new state, the United Principalities. In 1878, as a consequence of the war between Turkey and Russia, they were able to declare their formal independence. In 1881 Romania became a kingdom and Prince Carol took the title of Carol I.

Under the rule of Carol I, which was to last until the eve of World War I, Romania became a viable national entity. To the sense of nationhood was added substantial economic progress: the first industries were built, a national system of railroads was well along the way, and modern economic institutions were established. Completion of this first phase of nation-state building came in 1918 when, under the terms of the Versailles Peace Treaty, other areas where the Romanian-speaking population was a majority were added to the new state. Transylvania was the key new territory, but not the only acquisition: others were the Banat (to the southwest), Bucovina (to the northeast), and Bessarabia (to the east). Overnight the Romanian state more than doubled in size and population.

During this period politics remained conservative and authoritarian. Under the country's first constitution, that of 1866, a constitutional monarchy was established that made provisions for representative institutions. Within this context the country's first political parties came into existence. But in practice this was a government of minorities dominated by the landowning elite (the boyars) in which some provision was made for the participation of those tied to the country's economic development: a small, developing middle class and an even smaller group of industrial entrepreneurs. Although a peasant revolt broke out in 1907, the regime remained largely unchanged and the response to pressures for social change was outright repression.

The incorporation of the new territories, however desirable from the standpoint of nationalistic appeals, greatly increased the problems facing the Bucharest government. While the Old Kingdom consisted of territories east of the Carpathians where there was a strong sense of national identity based on a common culture, language, and religion and a shared history of common movements to establish autonomy, these appeals had little meaning westward, in Transylvania and the Banat. There the Magyar and German minorities had long constituted the dominant social, political, and economic groups and were closely identified with the institutions of Austro-Hungary, while the Romanian majority was largely a peasant population with a long history of submission and exclusion from political life. There were few native Transylvanian Romanians to whom the national government could turn for leadership in that area, yet the Magyar and German residents were clearly unacceptable in a new state defined in terms of Romanian nationalism. Furthermore, in contrast to their experience in the *regat*, the ruling elite found it necessary to make a conscious effort to redevelop a sense of Romanian ancestry among the peasantry. Thus, not only was there a serious leadership vacuum in these regions and the problem of newly subjected minorities who rejected the authority of the Romanian state, there were also the revisionist claims of Romania's immediate neighbors: Hungary for Transylvania, Bulgaria for Dobruja, and Russia for Bucovina and Bessarabia.

GOVERNMENT IN OLD ROMANIA

From its inception, the problems facing Greater Romania – the entity that had come into existence after World War I – were essentially unresolvable. Increased territorial size and population contributed to the fragility of the new state, rather than diminishing its problems of establishing and maintaining national cohesion. The Bucharest government was determined to share power in the new territories only with ethnic Romanians and pursued throughout this period a conscious policy of excluding minorities from participation and representation in the new state. The old system of governance in these areas had been equally repressive; what had changed was that the minorities who had held the power and ruled in their own interest for generations now found themselves subject to rule by those representing the Romanian majority.

Conservative Rule

To minimize divisions and to maximize the concept of a shared nationality among all Romanians, the instruments used most often to overcome these cleavages were chauvinism and anti-Semitism. Chauvinism was the appeal made to the Romanian population west of the Carpathians, emphasizing a distinctive culture and valorizing peasant society, and it advocated the exclusion of Magyars and Germans from participation in the new state on the grounds of incompatible ethnic and cultural differences. East of the Carpathians, anti-Semitism became the vehicle for nationalism, calling attention to the status of the Romanian Jewish community as an equally distinct minority in culture and traditions. If the Magyars and Germans west of the Carpathians were to be identified with old-regime bureaucrats, police, and privileged economic groups, eastward not only were many of the overseers of the estates Jewish but they formed a substantial and visible part of a small but increasingly important class of merchants, traders, and entrepreneurs. From the standpoint of the Romanian government the revisionist claims of Romania's neighbors and their identification with national minorities became useful as a rallying force for quieting dissension and justifying government policies. Throughout this period the first priority of the government was maintenance of Greater Romania's territorial integrity, rather than serious consideration of the economic demands made by the peasantry and a small but active working class.

The political elite of Old Romania, with its focus on the institution of monarchy and the French concepts of state and society, looked upon itself as the appropriate agent of modernization, ruling over a people who had to be forced along the road to Westernization. To the longstanding preoccupation with Russian influence over Romania and the absence of a well-defined border between Moldavia and Russia was added the fear instilled by the Russian Revolution and by Bolshevism after 1918. To offset these pressures, the government sought even closer identification with the West, especially France.

The Absence of Alternatives

Despite the conservative orientation of Romanian government in the interwar period, its restricted social base, and the lack of responsiveness to pressures from below for social change, an effective opposition did not emerge. The Peasant party began as a vehicle for antisystem groups, but its leaders were soon coopted by established political forces. Working within the framework of populist political organizations its party representatives found it much easier and more appealing to bargain with the leaders of the dominant Liberal party for participation in government than to press for reforms on behalf of the peasantry.

The Romanian Communist party, formed in 1921, was even less an appropriate instrument for change and protest during these years. From its inception to its outlawing in 1924 to its reorganization in 1944 as an organization at the service of the invading Russian armies, it lacked mass appeal. It was successful primarily among alienated minority groups. Despite the emphasis placed upon continuities within the Romanian Communist party (PCR) the prewar party organization, with its restricted base, was a very different organization from the mass-based organization created in the 1950s and 1960s.

The primary vehicle for the development of Marxist thought in Romania in this period was another left organization: the Socialist party (later known as the Social Democratic party). A small organization, antedating the formation of the PCR, it appealed to intellectuals alienated from the established order and to politically conscious workers, where they existed. Its primary contribution during these years was the development of a strand of Marxist thought compatible with Romanian nationalism, in contrast to the pro-Moscow and antinationalist stance of the PCR. To enter into a discussion of the Social Democratic party is to tread upon a very sensitive area—one that is poorly documented, poorly researched, and virtually closed to discussion for the last thirty years. Yet it is impossible to understand the nature of the present regime and the very different character of today's PCR without returning to these roots. While there are obvious and real differences in today's situation in Afghanistan and the formation of a pro-Moscow government in Romania after 1947, there are those Romanians who lived through these developments in prewar Romania, experienced the trauma of World War II and its aftermath within the confines of their country, and accommodated themselves to the building of national communism in the later years of the Gheorghiu-Dej regime and under the Ceauşescu regime. Their experience is one of forced accommodation, realization that the only hope for limited autonomy was acceptance of the primacy of Soviet influence, and negotiation within these constraints of a margin of independence.

Suffice it to say, documents in the restricted party history for the years 1934–1940 establish quite clearly the internationalist orientation of the prewar leadership of the PCR, in its willingness to negotiate and accept the dismantling of Greater Romania.[1] Equally valuable in separating this orientation from the attempt to develop a more authentic Romanian socialism are the pamphlets and publications of the Socialist party distributed primarily from Iaşi, beginning around the turn of the century.[2] The more legitimate heir to these ideas a half-century later was the new PCR built by Gheorghiu-Dej. It is here that one must draw a sharp dividing line between the earlier and the later party organizations, seek to understand the significance of the purging of Vasile Luca and Ana Paulker after the war and the development of national communism as the only viable route to a negotiated autonomy. But first there were two important developments: the country's experience with authoritarianism and the consolidation of a particular set of structures and behavior patterns identified with the imposition of a prefectural system.

Bureaucratic Authoritarianism

The pre–World War II Romanian state was essentially a bureaucratic-authoritarian regime characterized by a limited pluralism and dedicated to the exclusion of mass pressures. All the governments in power between 1918 and 1940 were faced with pressures for socioeconomic and political reform, but none responded effectively to the fact that large numbers of people were being mobilized and politicized. While nationalism was used as a device for building allegiance to the new state, it also became a vehicle for mass mobilization and agrarian demands. As conditions changed in the countryside and the peasantry reacted against conditions of neoserfdom, pressures built up for land reform. While some land redistribution did take place (14 million acres were eventually divided among some 1.4 million peasants) in no way did it respond to the desire for greater equity in land distribution and for improvements in rural conditions of life. Both the Liberal party (the "official" party) and the Peasant party (the recognized opposition) failed to serve as effective vehicles for responding to these demands, despite the fact that mass mobilization was underway throughout the country as a consequence of the granting of universal suffrage after World War I. The peasantry constituted by far the most important bloc of voters under these new political conditions.

Compounding the lack of meaningful political change to accommodate changes in the countryside were changes in the urban areas. Economic expansion after World War I produced benefits that were concentrated in the hands of a new middle class that identified itself with the Liberal party and was centered primarily in Bucharest. When the Peasant party first appeared on the scene in the late 1920s, it had the potential of bringing together a broad coalition of antisystem forces made up of the peasantry, intellectuals desiring change, the new professional classes, and the national minorities and others opposed to continued rule by the Liberal party. Yet, when the Peasant party captured power in 1928 and formed a government for the next three years, it failed to realize its potential. For all practical purposes, it became part of the factional, elitist-dominated political order centered in Bucharest.

As a consequence, while adjustments were made in the political system during these years, at no time was provision made for effective mass participation in politics. The regime was in this regard an instance of democratic formalism or controlled democracy, in which the system was continuously adjusted and manipulated to accommodate elite groups. If before World War I effective power was concentrated in the hands of large landowners, after the land reforms of 1918–1921 it shifted in the direction of those involved in industrial and financial ventures. Complementing this shift was growth in the size of the state apparatus and a subsequent rise in the number of individuals seeking employment in government, to man new state services and to serve as mediators between the government and those with the capital to invest in the Romanian economy. These capitalists were foreign firms and individuals (especially those of German origin) and Jewish nationals, who were the dominant element in the small but expanding entrepreneurial class. It was in this setting that politics, under the rule of Carol II (1930–1940), moved in an increasingly authoritarian direction.

Provincial Government

The bureaucratic-authoritarian character of the constitutional monarchy is best grasped by examining the system of governance set up to regulate the countryside: the prefectural system with its territorial units, in ascending order, of commune (rural as well as urban), *plasă* (district), and *judeţ* (county, province, or department). At the head of each unit was a single individual, designated as the representative of the national government within the area under his jurisdiction. At the communal level this was the mayor (*primar*) who was assisted by a local council. Representing him in each of the villages within the commune was another administrative official with the title of assistant or secretary to the village mayor (*ajutorul de primar satesc*). While local councils were elected from within the communities they served, all mayors were named by the Ministry of the Interior. Furthermore, to insure adequate control from the center there was a special organ set up in Interior to supervise local governmental activities: the Inspectorate-General for Administration (Inspectoratul General Administrativ). The definition of its legal responsibilities is particularly revealing: it was, to use the language of Decree Law 3.219 of September 1940, an organ providing guidance and control for all external services (i.e., field services) and local administration ("organ de îndrumare şi control a serviciilor exteriorare şi a administraţiilor locale ale Ministerului de Interne").

Parallel structures existed at the district and provincial level. For the former, the title used initially was subprefect and later *pretor*, a term that was considered to be more authentically Romanian. His functions were defined as those of the major governmental officials in the *plaşa*: he was considered the representative of the Bucharest government and the political head within the district ("este reprezentantul guvernului şi şeful din cuprinsul plaşii"). The code made further provisions for judical responsibilities: the *pretor* was to be assisted by a notary public (*notar*) and other functionaries as needed and was designated the local representative of the Ministry of Justice (Ministerul Public). The key figure in this whole system of hierarchical controls over local government was the prefect, who answered directly to the minister of interior and exercised widescale political and administrative powers over all political and governmental activities within the *judeţ*.

THE TIES BETWEEN PAST AND PRESENT

There are several reasons for entering into these legal and administrative details. First, in the opinion of Nistor Prisca, a leading contemporary constitutional law authority in Romania, the 1940 law provides the clearest statement of the prefectural system that operated in Romania from the end of the nineteenth century until 1950, when it was replaced by a Soviet-style system. Actually this system went through numerous changes, so many that it required legal experts to interpret the language of the law. One of the authorities of the period, Constantin Botez, for example, mentions in his *Noul cod administrativ* [The new administrative code] that the basic law of August 14, 1938, had by 1944 gone through eighty modifications and that, accordingly, he had found it necessary to publish an annotated edition incorporating all the changes over the years, to guide government officials in their actions.[3]

The years from 1944 through 1949 were transitional ones – they are the years of the occupation of Romania by the Red Army and the losing struggle to establish a liberal democratic system in the face of Soviet support of and preference for rule by the PCR. Yet the old prefectural system continued to operate. One by one old-regime prefects were replaced and as one approaches the year 1950, more and more emphasis is placed upon the local councils. Still, for quite a long time after 1940 the prefectural system continued to function as it always had: as a device for controlling the provinces and insuring their subordination to the wishes of Bucharest.

Another reason for entering into these details of administrative history lies in the similarities in the approach to local government across the years – except for the hiatus extending from 1950 to 1968, during which Soviet influence was paramount. The prefectural system was not entirely an instance of importing another institution from France during an era when so much of that which was French was seen as synonymous with modernization. The system had its origins in very old local government practices that had emerged east of the Carpathians, in what Romanians call the Romanian Nation or Homeland – the Țara Românească, with its three historic divisions: Oltenia, the Țara de Jos (literally the "Land Below" the Carpathian mountains to the southwest, or Muntenia), and the Țara de Sus (the "Land Above," to the northeast). There the *județ* had long been the basic unit of regional or provincial government. When the Ceaușescu regime wished to return to a more authentic form of local administration in 1968, it was to this earlier concept and practice that planners turned.

The use of traditional terms and concepts had a symbolic effect on the people. Romania's original organic law – *Regulamentul Organic* – approved by the tsar and later incorporated into the Basic Law of 1864—made provision for the establishment of a system of provincial government in accord with what tradition had established. While various changes occurred after 1864 and continued to be made through 1940, representing modernization and updating, there was always an important element of continuity. The first set of legal provisions gave responsibility for the naming of prefects to the prince, who was to select an official for each district from a list of two candidates per district, presented by local boyars and property owners to the Administrative Council, which in turn was charged with the responsibility of submitting the list to the prince for final selection. Later this system was modified and expanded through the creation of a Ministry of Internal Affairs, but the informal practice continued of consultation with local influentials (i.e., property owners), with sufficient control from above to insure that the system would be maintained in proper form and that final appointments would be made from the center. As the system of local government grew more complex, with the expansion in the size of the official state and in the number of government functionaries, further legislation was enacted specifying the administrative services that were to be provided at the local level.

After World War I basic guidelines stipulated that urban communes should have as a minimum the following: an administrative service, an accounting and bookkeeping unit, a unit for the keeping of civil records, a technical service, a health service (*salubritate*), a sanitary service (i.e., garbage collection, street cleaning, etc.), and a fire protection agency. In addition, local units were charged with responsibility for drawing up local plans for systematic urban growth and establishing a local planning commission—a *comisie planurilor de sistematizare*. The reason for mentioning these requirements is to establish the fact that the emphasis on planning and urban development so characteristic of the Romanian system of local government in the 1960s and 1970s was already in place in Old Romania, as part of the existing scheme and model set for the modernization of the countryside and the creation of urban centers.

Finally, while much is made later of the system of dual subordination and dual administration as a peculiarity of Marxist-Leninist practice, one should realize that similar concepts were also present in the pre-1950 system of local government. One line of authority (and the most meaningful) was administrative—hierarchical controls emanating from the Ministry of Internal Affairs; the other was a system of local councils and local elections with municipal and communal "presidents." After 1950, there were marked changes, basically the opening of government to popular participation. But while there was a fusion of administrative and political responsibilities, the formal units of local government, insofar as governmental action is concerned, remained primarily administrative. Local political affairs were first dominated by property owners and this influence was expressed through local administrative officials as well as councils; after 1950 the exclusive political instrument operating within the community was the local party organization. Yet, as before, effective political and administrative power was concentrated in the hands of a restricted set of individuals. Their social class origins may have changed but, despite the illusion of popular participation, they remained—as they always had been—local officials accountable to and representative of the national government, one which dictated from above all effective governmental policies and actions at the local level.

When the "new territories" were added to the dominions of the Romanian state in 1918, the prefectural system was automatically extended to the new areas. Even more so there than in the lands east of the Carpathians, it was a governmental system designed to control and regulate closely the local population. Selection of governmental representatives was restricted to Romanian nationals native to Transylvania and the Banat, and minority groups were automatically excluded. But as the Bucharest government was not always confident of the ability of those selected to carry out effectively the policies of the national government, close supervision from Bucharest was always maintained as a crucial component of the system. Yet although the system of domination had changed (representatives of the Austro-Hungarian state were gone and in their place were authorities identified with the Romanian state) the consequences for the local population were not a great deal different. Whereas before the local Romanian population had been subordinated to the authority of Magyar officials, the new officials spoke Romanian and saw their mission to be the development of a sense of national consciousness within the local Romanian-speaking population and an awareness of their identity with the larger Romanian nation.

It would be erroneous to leave the impression that the incorporation of the new territories was easily accomplished. On the contrary, documents and books written during the period emphasize the tremendous problems confronted by the national government in setting up a system of local government and administration that would function effectively. Romania was a unitary state—one in which power was markedly centralized—and the national government had to recognize the existence of four very distinct regions, each with a different institutional history that could not be changed at once. In the Old Kingdom, the *vechiul regat,* the basic law for regulating communal affairs and activities remained that of 1864, with its provisions for *judeţe.* In Transylvania, always referred to in Romanian parlance as the *Ardeal,* there was a

Magyar administration. In Bucovina, it was Austrian. In Bessarabia, local administration was an extension of the tsarist system of government established for the Russian Empire. Despite the desire to set up a common system of local government immediately, in accord with the model provided by the Old Kingdom, the transition took much longer than expected. In effect a uniform governing statute for the new Romanian state – Greater Romania – did not emerge until August 1929 and a common system of local government did not go into effect until March 1936.[4]

Even legalistically, the new state that emerged after 1918 was a very fragile entity. Once international pressures increased and the external power alignment in the region underwent modification, it had immediate and direct repercussions for the Romanian state and its definition as a geographical entity. Greater Romania was, and remained, a state in search of a nation.

NOTES

1. These documents are contained in the following publication of the Central Committee of the Romanian Communist party: *Istoria Partidului Comunist Român – sinteză – capitolul IV: Partidul Comunist Român, mişcarea muncitorească şi antifascistă din România în anii 1934–1940 – documentar* [A history of the Romanian Communist party – syntheses – Volume IV: The Romanian Communist Party, the working-class and anti-fascist movement in Romania during the years 1939–1940 – documents] (Bucureşti: Institutul de studii istorice şi social-politice de pe lînga CC al PCR, no date).

2. This statement is based on a series of confidential, informal interviews held during the time I was in Romania during 1977–1978 and is substantiated by a collection of reprints given to me dating back to 1884. They are as follows: "Karl Marx şi economiştiĭ noştrĭ" [Karl Marx and our economists] (Iaşi, 1884); "Evoluţie şi revoluţie" [Evolution and revolution] (Iaşi, no date [but since it is a reprint from *Revista Socială* No. 7, it is probably 1884]); Petru Kropotkin, "Cătră tinerĭ" [For young people] (Iaşi, 1886); "Ce vor socialiştiĭ romînĭ: expunerea socialismului ştiinţific şi programul socialist" [What Romanian socialists want: an explanation of scientific socialism and the socialist program] (Iaşi, 1886); Friedrich Engels, "Socialism utopic şi socialism ştiinţific" [Utopian socialism and scientific socialism] (Bucureşti, 1891); Karl Marx şi Friedrich Engels, "Manifestul Socialist" [The socialist manifesto] (Iaşi, 1893); and "Robiea şi socialismul" [Bondage and socialism] (Iaşi, 1893).

3. Constantin Botez, *Noul cod administrativ* [The new administrative code], vol. I (Bucureşti: Informaţie zilei, 1944), p. 3.

4. Erast Diti Tarangul, *Tratat de drept administrativ român* [A treatise on Romanian administrative law] (Cernauţi: Tipografia glasul Bucovinei, 1944), pp. 149–150. While there is no need here to belabor this point, detailed discussions of

the administrative difficulties encountered in incorporating the new territories are to be found in Aurel Onciul, *Organizaţia României Mari: studiu* [The organization of Greater Romania: a study] (Cernauţi: Tipografia Hermann Czopp, 1920); and Nicolae Cicu şi Ioan Alexandru, "Perfecţionarea continuă a aparatului de stat şi reflectarea sa pe plan legislativ" [Continuing improvements in the state apparatus and their reflection in the legislative plan], in Consiliul Legislativ, Coordonator: Ioan Ceterchi, *Dreptul românesc contemporan: evoluţie şi perspective* [Contemporary Romanian law: its evaluation and perspectives] (Bucureşti: Editura ştiinţifică şi enciclopedică, 1977), pp. 55-110. The latter article, in my opinion, contains the best single summary of Romania's administrative history encountered during research in Romanian libraries; it contains an especially useful summary of the difficulties encountered by the national government in incorporating the new territories.

2

The Destruction
of Old Romania and
the Construction
of a New Socialist Order

The years 1938 through 1950 were a traumatic era in the development of modern Romania. So great were the changes during these years that the nation and the state that emerged after World War II constituted a radical redefinition of the national society in formation during the nineteenth and early twentieth centuries. Once again the historic pattern of external circumstance combined with internal political disintegration produced regimes at the service of the powers dominant in the region. During the war years the regime could be classified as fascist; since then, except for a brief interlude between the departing German armies and the consolidation of the Soviet occupation, it has been Stalinist.

Fascism and Stalinism, each dedicated to the destruction of the other, undid what limited progress had been achieved over the previous century in building an independent and viable Romanian nation-state. In effect, national reconstruction in the full sense of the word – economic, social, political, and cultural – did not begin until the early 1950s and even then did not achieve full expression until 1958, with the removal of Soviet troops that summer and the declaration in November of the regime's commitment to the construction of its own version of socialist society. By 1968 Romania had come full circle, returning to terminology and concepts identified with the prewar territorial system of administration, now made compatible with the newer socialist reality, and had consolidated a state apparatus capable simultaneously of maintaining absolute control and engendering sustained socioeconomic growth.

Socialist construction, however, took place in a wasteland. Prior to the arrival of the Red Army, the Iron Guard movement, with its cult of anti-Semitism, violence, and fanatical devotion to a variant of Orthodoxy medieval in character, had already served as the catalyst to bring an end to a French-style constitutional monarchy and a nascent multiparty system. The establishment of a "royal dictatorship" in 1938, the abdication of Carol II in favor of his son Michael in 1940, and the subsequent rule of General Ion Antonescu in cooperation with German representatives of the Third Reich served to identify Romania solidly with the Axis cause during World War II. Romanian troops fought with the Germans on the eastern front. Faced with the loss of a substantial part of the new territories – first Bessarabia and northern Bucovina (to the Soviet Union) under the terms of the Soviet-German nonaggression pact and, shortly thereafter, southern Dobruja (to Bulgaria) and part of Transylvania (to Hungary) – Antonescu saw in an alliance with Germany not only the prospect of survival of core areas of the Romanian state but also a means of regaining land to the north and east.

The war years accelerated the process of disintegration. First Romanians had to contend with German hegemony and later, as the Axis powers collapsed, with the advance of Russian troops into Romanian territory. The consequence of Soviet liberation was the imposition of a Marxist-Leninist regime and Stalinist controls. During both eras of occupation there were obviously Romanians who cooperated with those who dominated their country, just as in other periods of subjugation there had been those willing to work with those who held power. But for most of the people – those who remained tied to the land and lived through these eras of occupation as armies swept through the countryside first from the west and then from the east – the experience was not unlike that of earlier times, the memory of which is best expressed in the oral tradition so much a part of Romanian folk culture. First one set of rulers imposed their order, then they were followed by another; in time a new leadership arose that sought to work within current constraints to reestablish as much national autonomy as possible under the circumstances.

The region where one can best capture a feeling for the national trauma tied up with these twelve years is Iaşi, both the province and the city. This is one of the country's core culture areas, yet a region where a limited number of landmarks remain from the prewar period. Here not only was the pattern of settlement affected by the changing lines of the eastern front, but its human geography also was much changed. Where there were once commercial and agricultural communities with a very old and lively Jewish-Romanian small-town culture, new towns are under construction. The city of Iaşi itself, the historic capital of Moldavia and long an important Romanian cultural center, had one of the largest concentrations of Jews in prewar Romania. Today its Jewish-Romanian culture is a question of history, identified only with a section of the city. Iaşi's Orthodox churches, monasteries, and public buildings constructed under the monarchy were equally affected by the war. Today, with the more important ones rebuilt and restored, they serve as vehicles for recapturing much of this region's past. Yet they stand adjacent to uniformly constructed factories and apartment buildings, which symbolize and give expression to the new industrialization and urbanization characteristic of postwar Romania. Dispersed in villages and small population centers and concentrated in the urban sprawl that has become contemporary Iaşi, the region's population is overwhelmingly Romanian. It is a provincial society at once both new and very old, and change is underway everywhere—extending outward from Iaşi across the rolling plains to small villages north and south facing eastward to the Prut River and the adjacent Moldavian SSR.

Before considering further the postwar changes imposed on Romania, one should understand how the prewar political system first decayed and collapsed. By most accounts, Carol II was a disaster. Leaving aside the personal scandals that characterized his court, it was his use of political power for personal advantage that proved to be so destructive. He used his political advantages as constitutional monarch to destroy political parties opposed to him, to coopt those politicians in the Liberal and Peasant parties amenable to his appeals, and to form and reform parliamentary governments to suit him. In 1938, faced with a direct challenge from the Iron Guard, he used the situation to declare an end to parliamentary government, arrested Corneliu Codreanu (the movement's leader), and established a royal dictatorship. From then until his fall from power in 1940, Carol II found himself increasingly isolated from within and from without. This was an era of growing German influence, economic as well as political, throughout the Balkans, and the decline of France as a viable ally on whom the country could rely. Faced with pressures from Russia for the reassertion of its sovereignty over Bessarabia and northern Bucovina, as well as from Hungary for Transylvania, Carol had no place to turn. Then, in a matter of weeks in June 1940, Greater Romania ceased to exist as quickly as it had been constituted; nearly a third of the newly constituted nation-state passed out of Romanian control. Affected by these changes were a population of some 1.6 million in northeastern Romania, 170,000 in Bucovina, and another 1.3 million in Transylvania.

Despite the power potential of the Iron Guard movement and its ability to mobilize mass support, it would be erroneous to say the military government of Antonescu was dominated by this organization.

Just as Carol II manipulated political parties to his advantage, Antonescu used the Iron Guard movement to displace Carol II from power and to establish his own personalist military dictatorship. Once he had consolidated his control, he quickly dispensed with the Iron Guard and contributed directly to its demobilization and demise.

With this background in mind, one must seek to understand something of the nature of the two movements in the Romania of that day with the greatest potential for mobilizing mass support: the right-wing Legion of the Archangel Michael (the Iron Guard) and the Romanian Communist party (the PCR).

ROMANIAN FASCISM

Prewar disillusionment in Romania with the ruling "liberal" establishment was much like that encountered elsewhere in southern Europe. Comprehension of this fact is a necessary first step in understanding fascism. As in Italy, Spain, and Portugal, liberalism was essentially a conservative political movement associated with economic and cultural modernization and coupled with the construction of a new nation-state in accord with economic and political models provided by France and Great Britain.

Liberalism Compared

In Italy, the Liberal party was the instrument for national unification and a creation of the intelligentsia and northern elites who desired a single state for all Italians under the leadership of the House of Savoy. The *risorgimento* was as much the creature of a minority of the Italian population as was the Europeanism of the liberal wing of the Romanian intelligentsia and the business community. Scattered throughout a series of independent kingdoms and duchies, these men wanted to create a new nation, identified with the mainstream of European life, by bringing all the people living on the peninsula into a single state. Their Romanian counterparts shared the same aspirations and confronted many of the same difficulties: a quiescent peasantry accustomed to a traditional life style well removed from modern Europe, a core state under a ruling house that had the potential to serve as the symbol for national unification, subjection of the region to Great Power intervention, and commitment to the discovery of a way to transcend the divisions that had long prevented the emergence of a unified nation-state.

In Spain and Portugal, despite the existence of much older national states and the legacy of an imperial past, liberalism and modernization were as much a part of their late nineteenth and early twentieth century experience as was the case in Romania and Italy. While Spain and Portugal had achieved formal unification centuries earlier (and in Portugal it could be said that the nation already coincided with the state), both were as far removed from the mainstream of European life as were Italy and Romania. Although the modernization process was much more conflictual in Spain – given the fact that the modernizing elite had to replace what had been a dynastic state with a nation-state binding together a diverse people – in both Spain and Portugal there was the same preference for constitutional monarchy as the chosen political vehicle, the same emphasis on economic and social change in accord with models provided by France and Great Britain, the same desire to defeat traditionalism in national life and to reject older styles of governance and ways of thinking. These factors produced equally strong movements supporting Europeanization. The notable differences among these four pre–World War II societies – such as the Portuguese and Spanish experiments with republicanism – should not obscure their similarities.

Fascism Compared

When disillusionment set in with liberal constitutionalism and the attempt to Europeanize their respective populations, in all four cases the traditional wing of the intelligentsia aligned itself with other elite groups in national society tied to older and more established ways of doing things. The consequence was the appearance of reactionary movements that sought to redefine national identity and produce a model for modernization drawn from within rather than from without. While the origins of these movements were similar in their appeal to a distinctive (largely mythical) national past that valorized national culture, they varied greatly in their ability to mobilize mass support.

The mix between elitism and populism thus was different in each. In Iberian fascism the mass movement element was always the weakest and tradition-oriented elites the strongest. In Italy, where the same equation was present from the beginning, Mussolini was far more devoted to triggering revolutionary change than either Salazar (Portugal) or Franco (Spain). Consequently, Mussolini built a mass movement that soon overrode the tradition-oriented, upper-class individuals who were a part of his original coalition, although later he had to return to them for support when his populist organization began to fall apart and his government started to disintegrate under the impact of the war. In Romania, as in Italy, mass-mobilization populism was an important component in the original movement. But Romanian experience differed from Italy's in that its mass movement never became synonymous with a regime, shaping and controlling the instruments of government. Ideologically, too, there were differences. Romanian fascism had more parallels with Iberian fascism in its appeal to traditional social and religious values and in the absence of those secular revolutionary symbols so much a part of Italian experience.

Picking up on the intense nationalism inherent in the formation of a Greater Romania, Romanian fascism's basic appeals were to chauvinism and anti-Semitism. The movement sought to build a homogeneous, closed, tradition-oriented national community focused around a shared language as the expression of Romanian culture and a common religion, representing a mystical or spiritual variant of Romanian Orthodoxy. Its extreme nationalism became synonymous with anti-Semitism, given the visibility of the Jewish community and its frequently privileged position in rural and urban areas. Romanian fascism began in Moldavia, especially in Iaşi, where all these themes could be identified with the structure and tensions of that isolated provincial society. Once an area considered to be a core part of the United Principalities and long identified with the defense of Romanian cultural values, Iaşi had become a backwater since the union with Wallachia, the establishment of Bucharest as capital, and the incorporation of Transylvania. It was a city without a solid economic base, other than its historic status as a governmental center. The creation of a unified Romanian state, the exodus of its writers and intellectuals to the new capital, and the diversion of scarce resources to convert Bucharest into a Western-style city modeled after Paris not only produced a decline in the region but also engendered a kind of arrogant provincialism in defense of traditional values. Add to this the open, shared frontier with Russia, the desire to keep Bessarabia (which was identified in Iaşi eyes with the formation and defense across the centuries of a distinctive Moldavian-Romanian culture), and a great fear of the Russian Revolution as a vehicle for destroying the existing society and reasserting Russian hegemony over the region, and it was not surprising that fanatical nationalism became identified with strong anticommunism. This identification was further reinforced by absolute devotion to Romanian Orthodoxy in opposition to the atheism identified with Marxist-Leninism. The final component, anti-Semitism, likewise struck a familiar theme in this region. The Romanian-Jewish community was especially visible in Iaşi province and city and throughout all of Moldavia. A distinct community with its own traditions, readily visible in commerce and trade and closely identified with popular stereotypes in Romanian folk culture, it provided a ready scapegoat.

The Distinction Between Movement and Regime

Romanian fascism had its origins in a student movement of the early 1920s that soon took the form of a political party, the League of National Christian Defense. First established in 1923 by Corneliu Zelea Codreanu and Alexandru C. Cuza, the league amassed sufficient support by 1926 to enable it to capture six seats in the parliament. In 1927 Codreanu and Cuza split and Codreanu went on to found a new organization, the Legion of the Archangel Michael. More commonly known as the Iron Guard, it was a fanatical movement in all respects; Codreanu emphasized the values of personal dedication, sacrifice, and willingness to give one's life in service of the cause. In 1932 the legion gained five seats in the parliament. At that point the government reacted and declared it an illegal organization. Subsequently the legion underwent reorganization and reappeared as a movement called All for the Fatherland. Under that name, in 1937 it captured 16 percent of the electorate and a corresponding sixty seats in the parliament. This made it second in size only to the Peasant party. Once again, in 1938, it was dissolved by the government and, under the royal dictatorship of Carol II, a virulent campaign to destroy the movement was conducted, in which many lost their lives. Despite suppression by force, the Iron Guard continued to assert its demands and to gain popular support. Ultimately, it brought down the government of Carol II and, with General Ion Antonescu as the new head of state, entered the government under the leadership of Horea Sima. Once Antonescu and the military had consolidated their power, they proceeded in early 1941 to eliminate the Iron Guard from the government. Where Carol failed, Antonescu succeeded in suppressing the movement and bringing it under control.

Not much is known about the Antonescu government. From what information is available in source material and from references picked up in conversations during my period of research in the country, it is probably best classified as a military government committed to maintaining the status quo. Rather than a regime of committed fascists, this was more likely a government of conservative nationalists faced with the reality of German hegemony and the need to work out an accommodation that would permit Romania's survival. Supporting this interpretation is the fact that Romania had the weakest resistance movement of any of the Balkan states. From the popular point of view both German and Russian control were unacceptable. In contrast, in neighboring Bulgaria, where the government was also closely aligned with the Axis powers, opposition was widespread. In Bulgaria cultural affinity, derived from a sense of shared Slavic identity coupled with revolutionary communism as a way to bring down the old class-based society, merged in the resistance movement with the identification of Russia as the liberator. Few Romanians saw resistance in these terms. Instead, most opted for acquiescence and minimal cooperation, hoping that the military outcome of the war would lead to the arrival of liberating forces from the West before the collapse of the eastern front and an advance from the East.

The arrival of Russian troops in Bucharest in 1944 changed

everything. The Antonescu government fell and nationalist forces converged in a desperate last attempt to consolidate a liberal democratic
regime under Michael II. From 1944 to 1947 official Soviet policy was
one of cooperation with the Allies and assertion that a popular front,
representing all major democratic forces in the country, would rule. In
the meantime, a search began in Romania for leaders and for a following
to move the Romanian Communist party to the forefront. The problem
was that to accomplish this a solid Romanian organization was needed
with which the masses might identify; the old PCR clearly could not provide the required leadership.

THE ADVENT OF STALINISM IN ROMANIA

To establish more clearly the nature of post-World War II transformations and the changing character of the Romanian Communist party
(the PCR), the most appropriate place to begin is by clarifying the
makeup of the prewar party organization, the role of the PCR in consolidating the new regime, and the extent of the changes imposed.

The Old PCR

In the available source material in English, frequent mention is
made of the fact that the PCR was originally a small organization,
numbering about 1,000, identified primarily with the national minorities
within Romania and not with the majority of the population. Romanian
source material, for the most part, says very little on the subject;
however, one set of party documents contained in the multivolume
documentary history published by the Central Committee does substantiate this observation, although the figure cited is a third larger. Party
records for the year 1933 report 1,665 members,[1] distributed according
to nationality in the following manner:

Magyars (Maghiari)	440
Romanians (Romani)	375
Jews (Evrei)	300
Bulgarians (Bulgari)	140
Russians (Ruşi)	100
Moldavians (Moldoveni)	70
Ukrainians (Ucraineni)	70
Others (Ceilalţi)	170
Total	1,665

During these years the national organization was further divided, as it is today, on a regional basis. But, whereas today's party organization follows *judeţe,* or regional political demarcations, the prewar party followed the historic regional divisions out of which Greater Romania had been built. Regional membership figures in 1933 were reported accordingly.

Transylvania (Transilvania)	600
Bessarabia (Basarabia)	300
Moldavia (Moldova)	205
Bucharest (Bucureşti)	170
Dobruja (Dobrogea)	150
Bucovina (Bucovina)	140
Prahova (Prahova)	70
Oltenia (Oltenia)	30
Total	1,665

Most interesting of all, however, are the categories used in these documents, dividing party membership between the Old Kingdom and the new territories. Party parlance of the period refers to the latter as "occupied regions," *regiunile ocupate,* as opposed to *vechiul regat.* These records also give further support to the interpretation that the party was weakest in those areas where ethnic Romanians were the strongest:

Vechiul regat	475
Regiunile ocupate	1,170

Yet another breakdown of these figures distinguishes Romanian from non-Romanian membership. This particular information, which is contained in a table titled "The Old Kingdom and the Occupied Regions — National Composition," shows the following:

România:	Români	268
	Others (Ceilalţi)	270
Transilvania:	Maghiari	400
	Others	200
Basarabia:	Moldoveni	70
	Others	230
Bucovina:	Ucrainieni	70
	Others	70

Thus, not only was the prewar organization overwhelmingly identified with the non-Romanian component of the population, it did not see the occupation of the new territories as legitimate. Elsewhere in these documents reference is made to the negotiability of sovereignty over these areas and in these tables this mentality is captured in the labels used: "occupied" territories, rather than "new" territories, which was the more accepted term in other materials dealing with this period.

The PCR During the Transition

The leadership of the prewar party organization spent the war years in Moscow. With the arrival of the Red Army, they returned to Romania and immediately began to work on two objectives: the establishment of rule by the PCR over the country and the development of a wider, more encompassing party organization. The years from 1944 through 1947 were transitional ones in which the Soviet Union followed a policy of placating the United States and the Allies by supporting the establishment of a popular front government, while working internally with Vasile Luca and Ana Paulker to develop a new party organization and a mass following that would substantiate their claims that the most legitimate organization to rule postwar Romania was the PCR.

Needless to say, the Romania that emerged after the war was a very different entity from prewar Romania. Romania had begun its trajectory as an independent nation-state in 1878 with a population of 4.5 million. With the acquisition of the new territories in 1918 the population jumped to nearly 18 million, only to decline precipitously during the war with the separation of these territories. After the war – with Transylvania restored to Romanian sovereignty and southern Dobruja, Bessarabia, and northern Bucovina no longer under Romanian rule – Romania's population numbered some 16 million. Whereas the prewar state maintained a distinction between the Old Kingdom and the new territories and followed a French-style prefectural system of territorial organization, the new state replicated Soviet institutions. In place of *judeţe* (provinces) and *tinturi* (administrative regions, which existed in form only) one found from 1950 to 1968 *raions* and *regiune*. Most important, the Romanian Communist party quickly established its control of the state apparatus and allocated to itself exclusive political legitimacy.

Under the government of Petru Groza (February 1945 through December 1947), politics moved from a coalition government in which the PCR had representation to one in which the PCR was clearly in the majority to a PCR monopoly. Symbolizing the end of this transition was King Michael's abdication on December 30, 1947, and the declaration of Romania as a people's republic. Accompanying these changes in territorial size, regional administration, and political transformation were equally great socioeconomic transformations: basic land reform, nationalization of the economy, and the formation of joint Soviet-Romanian companies (Sovroms). In place of the mixed economy characterizing prewar Romania – with its industrial enclaves and large landed estates amidst small landholdings – a highly centralized planned economy emerged, focused around republican industries and state farms and cooperatives. Along with these revolutionary changes in state and society there were substantial modifications of the core administrative apparatus of the state. To the original group of central ministries, formed well before the war, a state planning apparatus with oversight authority and an ever expanding number of economic ministries with command responsibilities were added.

The Extent of the Changes

As might be expected, there were immediate and revolutionary changes in the social class and professional background of the country's professional politicians. In the National Assembly, a new political class quickly replaced the old. One index of this transformation can be found by comparing the National Assembly before the war (a bicameral body) with the assembly after the consolidation of Soviet-style government (a unicameral entity).[2] In the period from 1922 through 1937 – the era of greatest party competition and expansion in the electorate – 2,687 deputies and 1,544 parliamentary representatives served in the National Assembly. From the perspective of the PCR, these politicians represented exclusively the bourgeoisie. Examination of their professional backgrounds confirms this image to a substantial degree. There were 4,353 representatives.

1,544	lawyers (35.5 percent)
555	property owners (14.8 percent)
282	university professors (6.5 percent)
272	secondary school teachers (6.2 percent)
216	primary teachers (5.6 percent)
196	priests (4.5 percent)
181	higher church authorities (4.2 percent)
159	medical doctors (3.7 percent)
131	engineers and architects (3.0 percent)
127	newspaper people (2.9 percent)

In contrast, in the 1969 Grand National Assembly (the Marea Adunare Naţionala) there were 465 deputies.

265	working class (55.1 percent)
187	managerial personnel with dual respon-

sibilities in party and state organizations at the central and local levels and within mass organizations (40.2 percent)

67   women classified as workers, peasants, or intellectuals

62   minorities (Magyar, German, Ukrainian, Serbian, Jewish, etc.)*

There are several problems with these figures, regardless of how helpful they are in contrasting the makeup of the pre- and postwar parliamentary leadership and despite the fact that, alone of the materials obtained in existing Romanian library sources, they permit comparison. The prewar figures give professional and work backgrounds of only 3,663 of the 4,353 members listed and account for only 86.9 percent of the occupational activities. Since the primary source used was Mattei Dogan's study of prewar parliaments (i.e., the work of an émigré) and the original study is not readily available in Romania, one is probably safe in concluding that the missing 13.1 percent are of peasant and working-class background. As for postwar figures, they give a breakdown for only a single legislature and these account for 452 of the 465 deputies—those who were working-class members engaged in production and managerial roles. Of the 465, 67 were women and 62 were minority representatives. What is of interest here—apart from the working-class background of a majority of the deputies, which one might expect to find—is the underrepresentation of women (14 percent of the national assembly), the separate status accorded to minorities (and the categories of the population included in these figures), and the separation of managerial functions from nonmanagerial functions.

Given the nature of the "revolutionary breakthrough"[3] established by 1950, with its implantation of a Stalinist regime and a Marxist-Leninist ideology, there is no need for an extensive documentation of the political, social, and economic changes carried out. All representatives of the old political class were removed from office; the socioeconomic base of the bourgeoisie was destroyed; nationalization of the economy was complete by the end of 1948; and an elaborate system of state farms and cooperatives was mounted in imitation of the Soviet example. However, further insight into what "revolutionary breakthrough" means in practice can be gained by using agriculture as an example.

Agricultural Transformation

As was the case with the Soviet Union, while it was relatively easy

---

*Note: figures not internally consistent; see Drăganu, p. 317.

to remove the old landed elite, collectivization of land held in small plots by peasant families took much longer. Here transformation of the countryside required some fifteen years, from 1950 through 1965. According to the most reliable source on the topic, the work of the rural sociologist Mihail Cernea, Romania moved from some 3 million small producers in 1950, occupying approximately 8 million arable hectares divided into more than 20 million plots, to a collectivized agriculture in the early 1970s that consisted of a network of 4,680 cooperative farms, involving 3.4 million peasant families (95 percent of the total) and 94 percent of the arable land.[4]

For what was a predominantly rural society, transformation of landholding patterns, affecting large as well as small properties, entailed major social change. Some of the dimensions of this change can be captured by comparing the data in Tables 2.1 and 2.2. Yet, the complete picture is not available in these figures. While there is ample discussion of the establishment of agricultural cooperatives, as evidenced by the data in Table 2.1, information on state farms (Intreprinderi Agricole de Stat, IAS) is notable by its absence, except for the most general of references.

TABLE 2.1

LAND TENURE IN PREWAR ROMANIA

Size	Number of Units	%	Area(Hectares)	%
Under 5 Hectares				
0-1 ha	610,000	18.6	320,000	1.6
1-3 ha	1,100,000	33.5	3,200,000	11.1
3-5 ha	750,000	22.9	3,015,000	15.3
Subtotal	2,460,000	75.0	5,535,000	28.0
5-10 hectares	560,000	17.0	3,955,000	20.0
10-20 hectares	180,000	5.5	2,360,000	12.0
20-50 hectares	55,000	1.7	1,535,000	7.8
50-100 hectares	12,800	0.4	895,000	4.5
100-500 hectares	9,500	0.3	2,095,000	10.6
Over 500 hectares	2,700	0.1	3,375,000	17.6
Total	3,280,000	100	19,750,000	100

Source: 1930 Census as cited in Miron Constantinescu, Henri H. Stahl, Ion Dragan et al., Urban Growth Processes in Romania (Bucharest: Meridiane, 1974), p. 25.

TABLE 2.2

COLLECTIVIZATION OF ROMANIAN AGRICULTURE

Year	Type of Organization	No.of Units	No.of Families	Arable Land Affected
1949	CAPs (Cooperatives).........	56.........	4,000	0.1%
	Agr. Assns. (intovarasirca)[*]..	0.........	0	0%
1951	CAPs	1,089........	75,400....................	3.2%
	Agr. Assn.	0.........	0.....................	0%
1953	CAPs.......................	1,997........	169,000	} 11.9% **
	Agr. Assn...............	2,026........	102,000.................	
1954	CAPs.....................	2,070........	178,000................	} 13.0%**
	Agr. Assn...............	2,833........	139,000................	
1955	CAPs.....................	2,152........	183,200.................	9.5%
	Agr. Assn...............	4,471........	206,000.................	4.7%
				(14.2%)
1957	CAPs	2,755........	375,100....................	16.6%
	Agr. Assn..............	11,853.......	1,078,200....................	23.4%
				(40.0%)
1959	CAPs....................	3,745........	842,900....................	32.3%
	Agr. Assn..............	11,565.......	1,775,400....................	36.7%
				(69.0%)
1960	CAPs....................	4,857.......	1,416,000....................	50.3%
	Agr. Assn..............	8,828.......	1,567,200....................	30.7%
				(81.0%)
1961	CAPs....................	6,424.......	2,050,981....................	70.2%
	Agr. Assn..............	6,677.......	1,080,553....................	22.4%
				(92.6%)
1962	CAPs....................	5,398.......	3,294,800.................	91.0%
	Agr. Assn..............	1,317.......	214,800.................	1.8%
				(92.8%)
1965	CAPs....................	4,680.......	3,409,100.................	94.1%
	Agr. Assn..............	120.......	56,800.................	0.1%
				(94.2%)
1972	CAPs....................	4,549.......	3,452,500.................	94.1%
	Agr. Assn..............	0.......	0	0%
				(94.1%)

* These associations are described usually as a simpler type cooperative arrangement.
  They were eventually phased out.

**Breakdown not available.

Source: Mihail Cernea, "Curs de sociologie rurală. Uz intern. Partea I: Sociologie
cooperativei agricole de productie" [Course in rural sociology. Internal use.
Part I: The sociology of agricultural cooperatives] (Bucuresti, 1974),
pp. 106-107.

Equally difficult to evaluate is the proportion of land remaining under private ownership. Combining the available documentary materials with field trips through various parts of the countryside, what is certain is that the vast majority of agriculture in Romania is structured today in the form of agricultural cooperatives that are internally divided into individual farms. Cernea attributes to agricultural cooperatives 90 percent of the national territory, 75 percent of the country's production in cereals, 70 percent of its vegetables, and 36 percent of its meat.[5] Servicing them are tractor and farm machinery stations (Stațiune de Mașini Agricole, SMA) in those rural communities that are district administrative centers.

Current Romanian sources attribute less than 1 percent of the arable land to private ownership. If this figure is added to the 94.1 percent farmed through cooperatives (see Table 2.2), then state farms probably account for 5 percent of the cultivated land. But against these figures must be weighed other areas where private ownership continues, how these are classified in terms of arable land, and what percentage of agricultural production takes place on the state farms (IASs). It is general knowledge that the state has declared mountainous and hill areas of the country outside the realm of required collectivization. But here precise figures are unavailable and there is no way to compare these land units – in terms of the arability criterion – with those available for the cooperatives (Cooperative Agricole de Producție, CAP). What is certain is that this area is a sensitive one and that the peasantry has not readily accepted collectivization. In the north, east and west of the Carpathians, the peasantry continues to resist forced reordering (sistematizare) of the countryside – the relocation of the population into carefully regulated larger rural communities with uniform structures and abandonment of traditional signs of social differentiation as represented by size of dwelling and elaborateness of design and woodwork.

At the opposite extreme are the state farms, belonging to the sector known as state agriculture (agricultură de stat). Like republican industries, which are directly accountable to central government economic ministries, these entities are administered from Bucharest and bypass the regional chain of command used for the CAPs and local industries. Paralleling the CAP structure, they too are subdivided into individual farms.[6] They are found especially in zones of extensive agriculture, notably in cereals production. In contrast, substantial production of vegetables, fruits, and meat takes place on private plots – either on terrain set aside for individual family use on the CAPs or in areas exempted from collectivization. From the standpoint of the Romanian consumer these products are generally considered to be of a higher quality and regarded as more desirable and worth the time spent waiting in lines when they do appear.

Industrial Transformation

In building a new socialist order, urbanization and industrialization of the country through the creation of a command economy has been even more important than transformation of the countryside. Aggregate data record these shifts in terms of rural-urban differences, population engaged in agriculture and forestry as opposed to industry, and percentage of national income derived from the two sectors. This information is summarized in Table 2.3. What it confirms is the shift in Romania from a prewar underdeveloped agricultural economy with limited enclaves of industrial development to a postwar developing economy with an expanding industrial base and ever increasing urban population. Linked to these changes has been the planned growth of existing regional urban centers and the development of new towns, to avoid excessive concentration of resources and population in the nation's capital. Thus, by 1972, of the 8,589,566 people recorded as urban residents that year, 6,984,373 were located in 77 towns with populations over 20,000 and the remaining 1,606,193 in 159 smaller towns, of which 38 constituted newly declared urban communities.[7] Accompanying these shifts in population and economic development has been rapid growth in literacy to a point where the state claims 99 percent literacy.

TABLE 2.3

SOCIOECONOMIC TRANSFORMATION OF ROMANIA

Years	% Pop.Urban/Rural	% Pop. Employed in Industry/ Agriculture & Forestry	% Natl. Income from Industry/Agr. & Forestry
1938	21.4/78.6	7.9/76.7	30.8/38.5
1948/50	23.4/76.6	12.0/74.1	44.0/28.0
1955/56	31.3/68.7	13.1/69.5	--
1960	--	15.1/65.4	44.1/33.1
1965/66	38.2/61.8	19.2/56.5	--
1972	41.6/58.4	26.1/44.0	57.1/21.7

Source: Various statistical yearbooks of the Socialist Republic of Romania as cited in Miron Constantinescu, Henri H. Stahl, Ion Dragan et al., Urban Growth Processes in Romania (Bucharest: Meridiane, 1974) pp. 25, 36, 52, 65. Dashes indicate that percentages have not been provided.

TRANSFORMING THE STATE APPARATUS

An equally important part of the building of a new socialist order, but much less well known and more difficult to document, is the transformation and modification of existing state structures. This area is murky in almost any contemporary society confronting rapid change. If, on the one hand, revolutionary breakthrough does entail a rupturing of preexisting social, political, and economic forms of organization, on the other hand all contemporary governments have to confront the provision of basically the same kinds of services. Certainly there is a difference in the scope of these services and their inclusiveness, but in Romania – as in other middle-range developing countries – one finds a common set of institutions focused around three core domestic activities: budget and control, economic development programs, and social services. In Romania, as elsewhere, the imperative of centralization and control has produced large-scale, complex hierarchical organizations identified with the key institutions of the state, under capitalism as well as under socialism.

Central Government Alterations

The advent of Stalinism in Romania can be identified with two types of change in state administration: replacement of existing personnel with persons identified with the Romanian Communist party and organizational restructuring in accord with new governmental responsibilities and activities. The personnel problems facing the PCR were twofold: an excess number of state employees, as a consequence of the legacy of using bureaucratic positions to employ marginal members of the bourgeoisie, and the need to place party members and activists in positions of coordination and control. Insight into this process of change can be gained through two doctoral theses prepared at the party's Ștefan Gheorghiu Academy, where the students concerned were given access to Central Committee records and files: Ștefan Lache's "The Work of the Romanian Communist Party in the Democratization of the State Apparatus for the Period March 1945–December 1947" and Traian Caraciuc's "The Work of the Romanian Communist Party in the Area of State Construction for the Years 1948–1950."[8]

Much like the leadership in other developing countries with an extensive state apparatus, the PCR in 1945 found itself faced with a situation in which the majority of the budget was devoted to the payment of salaries to public functionaries; the figure cited is 75 percent. The party's initial response was to decree an immediate reduction of 25 percent in the number of state employees.[9] According to party calculations, by 1929 Romania had 450,000 public functionaries (a ratio of one public employee per each 34 inhabitants), a higher ratio – they stated – than that in Italy, Poland, Japan, Switzerland, or Bulgaria that year. A decade later, the number of state employees had increased by 19,000.[10] From the party's point of view a high percentage of these employees – especially those employed after 1929 – were legionnaires (i.e., members of the Iron Guard movement). Thus, profascist, ideological grounds alone were deemed sufficient for extensive purging of the public service. Accordingly, the Council of Ministers decreed that in 1946 the number of state employees was to be reduced by another 25 percent. At the same time, to reward those cooperating with the changes and to create incentives for more productive work, legislation was passed raising salaries and pensions for public employees by 100 percent.[11]

Coupled with these actions was the decision to increase the number of PCR representatives in state administration. Reflecting the party's evaluation that the Ministry of Interior was a key organization and that control of the existing system of territorial administration was essential to consolidation of PCR control, was the incorporation of 4,875 "activists" into the ministry in August 1946 and another 4,911 the following month. At the same time the total number of employees in that ministry and its dependencies was reduced by 30 to 40 percent. According to party records cited by Lache, these figures can be compared with a total of 3,445 party members placed in the other central government ministries (except for the War Ministry). Another example given by Lache in his discussion of these purges and the blanketing in of the party faithful concerns the placement of 3,000 party members in the mayor's offices in Bucharest by January 1946.[12] He goes on to state that at a plenary meeting of the party that same month it was decided to reduce the number of state employees since, it was said, there were still more than 100,000 excess personnel on the public payroll.[13] A May 1947 Council of Ministers decree issued a call for a further reduction in the number of state employees, this one amounting to 30 percent. By the end of that year, it was felt, the last bourgeois representatives had been successfully removed and the state apparatus was thus in accord with the National Assembly's declaration of Romania's status as a people's republic.[14]

Yet the party found itself saddled with the problem of administering a vast range of services in an economy that was now nationalized and in which a major commitment had already been made to collectivization of the countryside. Furthermore, despite the rapid growth in party membership during these years, it was neither feasible nor desirable to think of a state apparatus that would be synonymous with 100 percent party membership.

By 1950 the number of public employees had been reduced to a figure approximating prewar figures. The party reported a total of 439,434 public functionaries, of whom 210,633 (47.9 percent) had been placed in their positions since August 23, 1944, and the majority of whom had received promotions during the 1948–1950 period. Those who were of working-class background numbered 59,330 (13.27 percent) and 127,923 (29.11 percent) were recruited from the peasantry. Another 206,650 (47.03 percent) were drawn from what was termed "professional bureaucratic backgrounds"—i.e., persons accustomed to state employment. The remaining 46,331 (10.59 percent) belonged to "other categories."

While there is some discrepancy in these figures, between the total number of 439,434 public functionaries and the figure (439,234) cited for central ministerial organizations that same year (1950), what is of note is the number of party members in state administration: 148,349 (33.76 percent of state employees) for the year 1950.[15] Yet, in discussing the increase in the number of party members in administration longitudinally, Lache reports much smaller figures for the years immediately preceding: 7,710 for 1948, with an increase to 12,732 in 1949.   If these figures are reliable, along with the supporting documentation Lache provides in his footnotes from Central Committee records, they indicate an enormous turnover in public employees during these years. Such a wholesale removal of previous public employees first (1946–1947) followed by the blanketing in of thousands of new recruits identified with the party cadres (1949–1950) documents a determination to establish party control of the state apparatus quickly and decisively.

Accompanying these changes in public personnel was widescale institutional reorganization of the central government. These reforms got underway immediately after the formation of the Groza government in March 1945. One of the first acts of his government was the reorganization of the Council of Ministers in a way that gave Groza power to coordinate all departmental activities and to "rationalize" and "normalize" the public service. Both Lache and Caraciuc record in detail the institutional transformations between 1945 and 1948 and report their consolidation by the end of 1948 under a new constitution.[16] These changes, coupled with further modifications during 1949, meant that by 1950 extensive restructuring of the formal administrative apparatus, along with widescale utilization of new personnel, insured effective implementation of Soviet-style policies and patterns of party rule.

Provincial Government Changes

At the subnational level the changes imposed were equally revolutionary. Here it is easier to document what took place. In contrast to the piecemeal data and descriptive analysis provided by Lache and Caraciuc on central government reorganization, their discussions of local government are much more clear-cut. For example, Lache offers a comprehensive overview of the changes in territorial administration that were made to insure party control of the countryside and to destroy once and for all old governing structures.

To establish new lines of accountability between local and national governments two kinds of changes were made. First, leaving the previous institutional format intact, prefects, subprefects, mayors, and other minor officials outside Bucharest were replaced with representatives of the various parties, forming the post-1944 coalition governments. From 1945 through 1947, as the importance of the PCR increased at the national level, parallel adjustments were made at the local level, until PCR members were in the majority.

What is of note in these changes is the style of governance used in the Ardeal, the area west of the Carpathians. Whereas the prewar bourgeois leadership emphasized the use of Romanian personnel, the PCR – continuing along the lines established in its prewar organization – made extensive use of national minorities, especially the Magyar population. Tables 2.4, 2.5, and 2.6 summarize these changes. Equally important, but not included in these figures, was the immediate reorganization of the state's police apparatus and the gendarmerie (aparatul poliţial şi jandarmeresc).[17] Lache reported an increase in the size of the police force (jandarmi) from 1400 regular positions (posturi), in March 1945 to 1900 in January 1946, in the context of an overall increase in the jandarmi from 10,450 to 17,770 police officers.[18] In the "pacification" of the countryside the country police were "assisted" in the north of Transylvania by the Red Army, where a Soviet-controlled military zone was installed on October 24, 1944, and formal Romanian sovereignty reestablished March 13, 1945. The area affected covered eleven judeţe, in which Romanian officials were installed in all except the judeţe of Ciuc, Odorhei, and Trei Scaune, where the Magyar population was larger than the Romanian population.[19]

Throughout 1946 and 1947 further changes were made in local government personnel, so that by the time it was decreed that a Soviet-style system of local government would be imposed throughout the country, PCR control of existing local government institutions had already been established and the necessary personnel were in place to implement the new policy guidelines.[20] These changes were symbolized by an official change in terminology: the historic terms judeţe and consiliile populare were abandoned and Slavization of the language took place. The new terms were regiune, raione, and sfaturile populare. While

TABLE 2.4

PARTY IDENTIFICATION OF LOCAL GOVERNMENT PERSONNEL IN 1945

Position	PCR	PSD	FP	UP	PNT	PNL	UPM	Indep.	Total Positions
Prefects(judeţe)	9	10	9	10	7	10	3	0	58
Mayors of Municipalities, prov. capitals	10	12	9	9	2	11	2	3	58
Assistants for the above	14	17	10	9	11	23	2	2	83
Mayors of cities (oraşe)	15	20	7	4	8	16	5	5	59
Assistants for the above	13	18	5	7	7	16	4	0	70
Mayors of resort centers	4	4	3	3	3	5	2	0	25
Assistants for the above	4	5	3	4	0	4	1	2	22
Mayors of sectors within Bucharest	1	1	0	0	1	1	0	0	4
Mayors of communes dependent on Buch.	5	0	0	2	0	0	0	0	4
Assistants to mayors in the above communes	1	5	0	1	0	0	0	0	7

Total Party reps: 77.......93 ...36....51....39....86....19......13

Party symbols: PSD, Partid Social Democrat [Social Democratic party]; FP, Frontul Plugarilor [Plowmen's front]; UP, Uniune Patriotice [Patriotic union]; PNL, Partid National Liberal [National liberal party]; PNT, Partid Naţional Ţaranesc [Peasant party]; UPM, Uniune Populare Maghiare [Magyar popular union].

Source: Statistics from the Ministry of Interior for 1945 as cited in Ştefan Lache, "Activitatea Partidului Comunist Român pentru democratizarea aparatului de stat în perioadă marţie 1945-decembrie 1947"[The work of the Romanian Communist party in the democratization of the state apparatus for the period March 1945-December 1947], pp. 149-150.

such changes in language probably mean little to the outsider, they symbolized for Romanians the inauguration of eighteen years of tight Soviet control and forced reacculturation. Throughout the society, when a choice of words was available between a Latin-based term and a Slavic one, the Slavic word was preferred. *Sfat* and *consiliu popular,* for example, have identical meanings—local council—and this parallelism is widespread throughout Romanian, even down to the level of first names. Thus, institutional change identified with the advent of Stalinism went hand-in-hand with an attempt to make the country more Slavic and to force it into norms imposed elsewhere in Eastern Europe.[21] The

TABLE 2.5

NATIONALITY OF LOCAL GOVERNMENT OFFICIALS* IN THE ARDEAL IN 1946

Judeţe	Romanians	Magyars	Other Nationalities	Total
Satu Mare	263	243	59	365
Somes	177	44	6	227
Odorhei	6	213	1	220
Mures	173	474	2	649
Maramures	140	102	5	247
Cluj	277	311	10	598
Bihor	227	397	6	630
Cuic	2	84	0	86
Nasaud	186	23	0	209
Salaj	118	162	1	281
Trei Scaune	3	217	0	220
Totals	1,572	2,270	90	3,932

*Prefects and mayors of municipalities and cities with municipality status (orase).

Source: "Arhivele statului, Bucureşti, fondul MAI [Interior Ministry], dosarul nr.
60/1946" as cited in Ştefan Lache, "Activitatea Partidului Comunist Român
pentru democratizarea apartului de stat în perioadă martie 1945-decembrie
1947" [The work of the Romanian Communist party in the democratization of the
state apparatus for the period March 1945-December 1947], p. 173.

post-1950 system of local governments accordingly followed a format of 16 regions, 146 *raions,* and 180 cities (*oraşe*), in which Bucharest was given the status of a "republican city" (*oraş republican*). Another 39 cities received special status as regional capitals (*oraşele regiunale*); under their jurisdiction were 4,273 communes.[22]

CONCLUSIONS

By 1950 the institutional transformation of Romania, with its accompanying changes in state personnel, was complete. With the old regime decisively dismantled and previously dominant social classes removed, Romanianization of the party and the development of a mass organization could now proceed apace. Subsequently, what had been a minority organization became one that went to considerable lengths to identify itself with popular culture and to develop a mass following.

TABLE 2.6

INCREASE IN COMMUNIST PARTY AFFILIATION OF MAYORS IN SELECTED

PROVINCES (JUDEȚE) DURING 1947

Județe	PCR Mayors in Feb. 1947	PCR Mayors in Aug. 1947
Alba	13	75
Argeș	22	42
Buzau	0	19
Ciuc	10	19
Cluj	0	61
Dimbovița	59	75
Gorj	32	35
Fagaraș	13	23
Ialomița	21	25
Ilfov	30	45
Mureș	10	45
Nasaud	22	32
Odorhei	10	53
Prahova	21	45
Someș	7	87
Trei Scaune	29	32
Turda	22	58

Source: Arhivă CC al PCR, fondul nr.1, dosarul nr.9, filele nr.120, 123, Tabel cu date statistice pe lună august 1947 [Table with statistical data for the month of August 1947] , dosarul nr.7, fila nr.52, Table cu date statistice pe lună septembrie 1947 [Table with statistical data for the month of September 1947], Arhivele statului, București, fondul MAI [Interior Ministry], dosarul nr.35/1946-1947, fila nr.2, as cited in Ștefan Lache, "Activitatea Partidului Comunist Român pentru democratizarea aparatului de stat în perioadă martie 1945-decembrie 1947" [The work of the Romanian Communist party in the democratization of the state apparatus for the period March 1945-December 1947], p. 540.

Although official party figures record a mass following as early as 1947 of 704,857,[23] most accounts attribute these developments to the 1950s and the 1960s and to the rise of pronationalist leadership elements within the party in opposition to its more internationally oriented members, with their identification with national minorities. While both Gheorghiu-Dej and Ceaușescu were party activists during the 1940s, the leadership of Vasile Luca and Ana Paulker symbolized a very different kind of organization. Their removal became essential to the construction of a new image for the party and in the process a very different image of Romania as a socialist state was projected. The Romania of the late 1950s and the 1960s thus became, in the eyes of many, a regime with an independent foreign policy in which a degree of autonomy was possible and feasible in a way that proved to be impossible in either Hungary or Czechoslovakia. Was Romania, then, a "captive nation" as the émigré community asserted, or was it an independent socialist republic aligned with the USSR, with its own well-established, distinctive nationalist leadership, as its defenders claimed?

NOTES

1. *Istoria Partidului Comunist Român: sinteză—capitolul IV: Partidul Comunist Român, mişcarea muncitorească şi antifascistă din România în anii 1934-1940—documentar* [A history of the Romanian Communist party—Synthesis—Volume IV: The Romanian Communist party, the working-class and antifascist movement in Romania during the years 1939-1940—documents] (Bucureşti: Institutul de studii istorice şi social-politice de pe lîngă CC al PCR, no date), pp. 28-29. The discrepancy in totals between the first two sets of figures (1,665) and the second (Old Kingdom vs. new territories) is contained in the sources themselves. Also Romanian terminology used in the second two sets of figures has intentionally not been translated to illustrate the distinction these documents draw between ethnic Romanians and others.

2. The following discussion is based on figures quoted in Tudor Drăganu, *Drept constituţional* [Constitutional law] (Bucureşti: editura didactică şi pedagogică, 1972). See especially p. 317.

3. The phrase "revolutionary breakthrough" as it characterizes the extensive political, social, and economic transformations experienced by postwar Romania is adapted from Kenneth Jowitt's work, *Revolutionary Breakthrough and National Development: The Case of Romania, 1944-1965* (Berkeley: University of California Press, 1971).

4. Mihail Cernea, "Changing Society and Family Change: The Impact of the Cooperative Farm on the Peasant Family" (Stanford, Calif.: Center for Advanced Study in the Behavioral Sciences, 1970-71) (mimeographed), p. 26.

5. Mihail Cernea, *Sociologia cooperativei agricole* [The sociology of agricultural cooperatives] (Bucureşti: Editura academiei republicii socialiste România, 1974), p. 26.

6. For a detailed breakdown of these two agricultural sectors, see V. Hălmăjan, *Repartizarea teritorială a producţie agricole cu ajutorul metodelor economico-matematice* [The territorial distribution of agricultural production with the assistance of economic-mathematical methods] (Bucureşti: Editura ceres, 1977), p. 7.

7. Miron Constantinescu, Henri H. Stahl, Ion Drăgan et al., *Urban Growth Processes in Romania* (Bucharest: Meridiane, 1974), p. 109.

8. Ştefan Lache, "Activitatea Partidului Comunist Român pentru democratizarea aparatului de stat în perioada marţie 1945-decembrie 1947" [The work of the Romanian Communist party in the democratization of the state apparatus for the period March 1945-December 1947] (Bucureşti: Teză de doctorat,

Academia de învăţămant social-politic "Ştefan Gheorghiu" de pe lîngă CC al PCR, Facultatea de filozofie-istorie, 1970); and Traian Caraciuc, "Activitatea Partidului Comunist Român în domeniul construcţie de stat în perioada 1948-1950" [The work of the Romanian Communist party in the area of state construction for the years 1948-1950] (Bucureşti: Teză, Academia de ştiinţe social-politice "Ştefan Gheorghiu" de pe lîngă CC al PCR, Facultatea de Istorie a Mişcării Muncitoreşti, 1967), 2 vols.

    9. Lache, p. 130.

    10. Caraciuc, p. 251.

    11. Lache, p. 354.

    12. Lache, p. 368. He cites the following as his sources of information: Ministerul de Interne, Arhiva CC al PCR, fondul 1, dosarul 7, fila 50 – *Tabel cu date statistice privind organizaţiile de partid pe lună septembrie 1946* [Table with statistical data concerning the organization of the party for the month of September 1946] – and Municipul de Bucureşti, *ibidem,* dosarul 6, *Proces-verbal al sedintei plenare a CC al PCR din 25-28 ianuarie 1946* [Official report of the plenary session of the Central Committee of the Romanian Communist Party for January 25-28, 1946).

    13. Lache, pp. 351-354.

    14. Lache, pp. 532, 617.

    15. Caraciuc, pp. 255-256. His sources are: Arhiva CC al PCR, fondul 2, dosarul 113, fila 13; Arhiva Comitetului Orăşenesc PCR Bucureşti, dosarul 110, fila 333; Arhiva CC al PCR, fondul 2, dosarul 113, fila 1; Arhiva CC al PCR, fondul 2, dosarul 113, fila 13; Arhiva Comitetului Orăşenesc PCR Bucureşti, fondul 11, dosarul 101, fila 155; Arhiva CC al PCR, fondul 2, dosarul 1381/1394, fila 123.

    16. Lache, pp. 5, 10, 15, 17, 20, 54-55, 59-62, 67, 95, 100-101, 109-111, 442, 468-470; and Caraciuc, pp. 188-191, 214-221, 226-228.

    17. Lache, pp. 207-209.

    18. Arhivele Statului, Bucureşti, fondul D, dosarul 51, filele 17-22, as cited in Lache, p. 242.

    19. Lache, pp. 168-169, 172.

    20. Lache, p. 165.

    21. Detailed discussions of these institutional changes and the specific modifications made in territorial administration are amply presented in Caraciuc, pp. 105-109, 121-122, 129, 131, 133 and 139, and in Ioan Vîntu, Mircea Lepadatescu, Ioan Merelescu, and Mircea Anghene, *Sfaturile populare: organele locale ale puterii de stat în R.P. România* [People's councils: local organs of state power in the People's Republic of Romania] (Bucureşti: Editura academiei republicii populare Romîne, 1964), pp. 49-52, 200-205, 328-329, 346.

    22. Vîntu et al., p. 52. An official reordering of the territorial system of governance is to be found in *Indicator alfabetic al localităţilor din Republica Populară Romînă* [Alphabetical guide of localities in the People's Republic of Romania] (Bucureşti: Editura de stat pentru literatura ştiinţifica, 1954).

    23. Lache, p. 415.

Bucharest.   The university, founded in 1869, is on the right.

The dedication of Piață Obor, Bucharest.

Tower of the Old Council,
Sibiu.

A village home in Moldavia.

The market in Cluj.

A wedding in Arad.

The Iron Gates across the Danube.

Pioneers outside Pioneer Palace, Bucharest.

National Theatre and Romanian Opera House, Cluj.

Center of Arad.

Roman metope, Adamclisi.

Roman ruins, Istria.

Dragomirna Monastery, Moldavia.

Putna Monastery, Moldavia.

Peleş Castle, Sinaia.

View of the Carpathian Mountains.

Tower steps – Sibiu.

Shopping in Bucharest.

3

The Rekindling of Nationalism Under Socialism

Petru Groza's successor, Gheorghe Gheorghiu-Dej, was an equally faithful Soviet ally. As he consolidated his control of the PCR during the late 1940s and the early 1950s, Romania developed a full-fledged Stalinist political system and economy. Under his tutelage the balance of power shifted away from its older pro-Russian leadership toward Romanian nationalists, to those who shared an equally strong commitment to Marxist-Leninist principles but also wished to see a more thoroughly Romanian organization identified with historic aspirations for national independence. To carry out these changes Gheorghiu-Dej first had to demonstrate unquestioning orthodoxy and acceptance of Soviet preeminence within the socialist bloc. Once his position in the party was secure and his commitment to Stalinism unquestioned, he was able in 1952 to convince Stalin of the desirability of purges within the internationalist wing of the PCR and, when Stalin died in 1953, to move the regime in the direction of negotiated autonomy and greater control over its own internal affairs.

During these years there were essentially three important groupings within the party. The best known and most visible was the older, more internationally oriented faction that had provided the prewar leadership and had returned from Moscow after the war to implant a Marxist-Leninist regime. The names most frequently identified with it are those of Vasile Luca, Ana Paulker, and Teohari Georgescu. In their eyes the excesses of nationalism were identified with fascism and in building a new, multiethnic Romanian state, they sought to transcend the old sources of conflict through strong commitment to an international working-class movement. They favored developing a party organization that gave ample representation to non-Romanian elements. In Transylvania this involved Hungarian militants who had assumed an active role in the dismantling of "fascist" structures. East of the Carpathians it included those within the Jewish community with a strong

57

commitment to Marxist-Leninist ideals. The second group consisted of Romanian activists such as Gheorghiu-Dej and Nicolae Ceauşescu, who worked zealously during the late 1940s and throughout the 1950s to develop solid support among ethnic Romanians with working-class and peasant backgrounds. For them the development of a mass movement and mass organizations required the use of symbols and strategies closely identified with popular culture that would appeal to a broad cross section of the population. The third group involved a more cosmopolitan mix of intellectuals (intelectuali) and state and party bureaucrats (funcţionari). Closely identified with Miron Constantinescu and pro-Khrushchev forces within Romania and outside, these men supported relaxation of tight controls and a minimum of repression as the key to consolidating mass support and building a regime solidly identified with the diverse population and peoples of Romania.

In evaluating these groups, changing alignments within them, and their relative weight in terms of party organization as a whole, some idea must be given of the mass components of the party as it developed during the late 1940s and 1950s. There is considerable discrepancy in figures. One scholar, Stephen Fischer-Galati, credits the PCR with just under 600,000 members in 1955 and most external observers characterize the mid-1950s as the years during which a mass organization was developed. Official Romanian figures, however, place these developments earlier and give a figure of slightly over 700,000 (704,857, to be precise) as early as January 1947.[1] While one may question the accuracy of figures gathered so close to the end of the war and in the middle of the transition from a multiparty to a single-party state, it is certain that the late 1940s and the early 1950s marked an era of mass recruitment and the development of a much more broadly based party organization. If we accept these figures as a reliable representation of the party by 1950, they offer insight into its social base.

323,104 (45.84 percent)	workers
264,233 (37.48 percent)	peasants
43,465 (6.17 percent)	small handicrafts producers and small merchants
16,810 (2.39 percent)	intellectuals
52,525 (7.45 percent)	bureaucrats
4,720 (0.67 percent)	military[2]

During this period Gheorghiu-Dej was minister of industry and commerce and actively involved not only in the reorganization of the ministry (it later became two separate ministries) but also in mounting a centralized economic planning system and in organizing as wide a base as possible among industrial workers. Again, while there are discrepancies in the figures cited above and the breakdown given for bureaucrats in the previous chapter, where access to the original files is not possible, all that can be done is to call the reader's attention to these differences, signal the worker component as the largest portion of the party in these years, and point out its identification with Gheorghiu-Dej's leadership. During these years and immediately afterward Gheorghiu-Dej was the primary advocate for the country's economic policies: forced collectivization in agriculture, tight control of labor, and the setting of a high priority for industrial development.

KEY POLITICAL EVENTS

At the time of Stalin's death Romania was a Soviet satellite in all respects, closely integrated into the Eastern bloc politically, economically, and militarily. Furthermore, once he had purged the older leadership – especially Luca and Paulker – Gheorghiu-Dej moved not so much toward liberalization in the aftermath of Stalin's death as he did toward minimizing the influence of more cosmopolitan party elements that had responded to the Khrushchev reforms in Russia by issuing a call for similar changes in Romania. Consequently, Gheorghiu-Dej's immediate course of action was a continuation of Stalinist controls in economics and politics internally, while he began to loosen the external ties with the USSR that would perpetuate a relationship of dependency – economic, military, and diplomatic ties.

Negotiated Dependency

There were two phases in this development of negotiated dependency and autonomy: the adoption of what Gheorghiu-Dej termed a "new course" in 1953 and commitment to the construction of an independent socialist state from 1957 on. The essence of what was called the new course was the implementation of a set of policies designed to place the Romanian economy on a much more solid footing and to accelerate the development of as wide a range of economic autonomy as possible. Another way to describe these policies is to say that they entailed maximizing the values of economic nationalism: commitment to the industrialization of Romania, despite Soviet preference that the country focus on developing its agricultural, mining, and forestry potential for the benefit of the Eastern bloc as a whole and depend on others in the bloc for its needs in heavy industry. An immediate priority was the end-ing of joint economic ventures with the Soviets (the Sovroms) and diversification of Romania's external trade within and outside the bloc, to reduce the country's economic dependency on the USSR. While the push for greater autonomy did not become official until 1957, the objective of consolidating Romania's status as an independent socialist republic had been decided on much earlier and was always present in these calculations. Symbolizing the official commitment to a policy of autonomy within the Eastern bloc was Gheorghiu-Dej's appointment of Ion Maurer as foreign minister and his elevation to the position of chairman of the Presidium of the Grand National Assembly when Groza died in 1958. Coinciding with this declaration of the intent to pursue a policy of greater economic, military, and diplomatic autonomy within the context of the socialist camp was the withdrawal of Soviet troops in 1958 and the acceptance on the part of the Soviet Union of the desire of the Romanian leadership to exercise greater control over its own affairs.

By 1960 Gheorghiu-Dej had achieved even greater control over his country's internal politics by eliminating the remaining members of the pro-Moscow group from all positions of influence and by curtailing the influence of the "reformists"–those identified earlier as more cosmopolitan and flexible in outlook and more willing to adjust the system to gain wider popular support. From 1957 on, this wing of the PCR was, in Gheorghiu-Dej's opinion, too closely identified with Khrushchev and his supporters in the USSR and he perceived them as a direct threat to his own supremacy over the Romanian party and state. His policy of maintaining tight internal controls while shifting Romania's external alignments was facilitated by the Sino-Soviet split, which surfaced in the early 1960s. Not only did the Gheorghiu-Dej regime reject outright COMECON's[3] prescriptions for Romanian economic development but, once it failed to develop a mediatory role between Russia and China, it opted for strong support of the Chinese position. This departure was symbolized by two events in 1964: the sending of a Romanian delegation, headed by Maurer, to Peking and the April statement of the Romanian Workers' party concerning its official policy of autonomy and independence within the context of socialism. Since then the cultivation of close relations with China and the periodic exchange of official delegations has become an established component of Romania's foreign policy.

When Gheorghiu-Dej died in March 1965 he left implanted a most secure regime. Openly Stalinist in its internal style of governance, it had undergone considerable evolution since he first rose to power. Whereas the postwar Romanian leadership had had little if any direct control over internal policies and the country was clearly a Soviet satellite, Gheorghiu-Dej led the country away from direct Soviet control over national affairs. Never challenging for a moment orthodox Marxist-Leninist principles, he established quite clearly his support for the desire of so many Romanians for a government capable of setting its own internal and external policies.

Consolidation of the New Order

Gheorghiu-Dej's successor, Nicolae Ceauşescu, did not change these policies as much as he accentuated them, by giving greater publicity to the same objectives: secure internal control through maintenance of a very orthodox Marxist-Leninist organization, clearly dominated by the first secretary; maximum freedom to negotiate and set priorities for Romania's own internal economic development; the right to trade as much with the Western bloc countries as with the Eastern ones; diplomatic independence; and the exercise of an independent voice within Eastern European affairs on questions of an economic and military nature. From 1965 through 1967, while he was consolidating his own personal power, Ceauşescu followed a policy of relaxing internal controls. This relaxation led some observers to believe that significant changes were underway—that Romania was no longer a captive nation but was becoming an independent socialist state with a new leadership in full control of its own internal affairs, although committed, as was Cuba, to the advancement of international socialism and to cooperation with the Soviet Union when common interests were threatened by capitalist countries. Once Ceauşescu's position was secure, by 1968, it became apparent—as it had been under Gheorghiu-Dej—that the emphasis on an independent foreign policy bore no relation to internal affairs. A new set of tight internal controls replaced the old ones and there was the same commitment to Marxist-Leninism as defined by the Soviet Union. There was, in effect, a tacit trade-off between the two countries: in exchange for Romania's willingness to follow what was essentially a Soviet interpretation of Marxist-Leninist orthodoxy and recognition of Soviet supremacy in the Eastern bloc, the Soviet Union would tolerate nationalist rhetoric designed to create the illusion of national autonomy and would accept the Romanian desire to set its own internal development policy, even to the point of expanding its economic ties with the West. So secure was the Soviet Union's position economically in relation to Romania that multilateralization of trading patterns and economic relationships did little to change the fundamental reality of Romania's economic dependency on the Soviet Union.

Several events during these years highlighted these developments. In July 1965, on the occasion of the PCR's Ninth Congress, it was announced that, with the transition to socialism now complete, the country was not only a socialist republic (rather than a people's republic) but also – to reassert the country's Latinity – the official spelling of the country would henceforth be Romania rather than Rumania. Accompanying these changes was an acceleration of the removal of overt signs of Russian influence: the substitution of Romanian for Russian names on streets and buildings, the downplaying of the teaching of Russian and the upgrading of instruction in English, the phasing out of various Soviet cultural activities, and the encouragement of multilateral cultural contacts with other countries, including the United States, West Germany, and China. The following summer Ceauşescu attacked Soviet control of the Warsaw Pact's military forces and policies, proposing the dissolution of both the Warsaw and NATO pacts. Yet, while he pursued a diplomatic policy of diversification in Romania's foreign relations, he also took measures internally, as had his predecessor, to insure that his rule would be unchallenged. Thus, while he criticized Soviet actions to end liberalizing trends in Czechoslovakia, he moved against similar reformist forces in his own regime by removing from the party's Presidium leaders identified with the more cosmopolitan and reformist wing of the party: Chiva Stoica and Gheorghe Apostol. In so doing he accomplished both consolidation of his supremacy and curtailment of potential Soviet criticism of "deviation" from Marxist-Leninist orthodoxy, the grounds used to justify the dispatch of troops to Prague. Along with these actions was the further expansion in the PCR's official membership, which reached 1.7 million, according to his 1967 report to the annual party congress.

Ceauşescu's 1967 party report called attention to two important accomplishments: consolidation of the party's status as a mass organization and institutionalization of a regime of national communism. Just as the imposition of Soviet-style field administration and local government organization in the 1950s symbolized the era of maximum Russian influence over Romania, alteration of the system of territorial organization – announced at this party congress and implemented in 1968 – captured the mood of the early years of the Ceauşescu government: the consolidation of a Romanian socialist republic and the building of national communism. The very title of that year's report, delivered by Ceauşescu, gives expression to these policies: "Report concerning the Measures for Perfecting the Management and Planning of the National Economy and for Improving the Administrative Territorial Organization of Romania."[4]

In addition to the change in language, whereby Russian terminology was replaced with more authentically Romanian terms (*judeţe* as the sole provincial or regional unit in place of two levels, *regiune* and *raione*), there was replication of the lines of authority at the provincial and local level of what Ceauşescu had already established at the top – the fusion of state and party roles. In accordance with his dual status as president and first secretary, it was decreed that at the provincial and local level the same fusion would occur, with each major executive official becoming simultaneously president of the appropriate people's council and first secretary of the parallel party organization.[5] At the national level, Ceaușescu sought to increase the responsibilities of official governmental organs while perfecting the fusion between state and party organizations. To paraphrase further from his 1967 report, the Grand National Assembly was to function as the supreme organ of state power; the State Council was charged with the responsibility for assuming a much more active control over the way the regime's laws and decisions (as passed by the assembly) would be implemented; and the Council of Ministers was defined as the ultimate authority over state administration and as the party's principal agent for implementing its policies.[6]

The primary characteristic of this report, and of subsequent actions by Ceaușescu in dealing with state power, is the emphasis on rationalizing and perfecting the existing institutional apparatus, in accord with a Romanian model for the construction of socialist society. Under Ceaușescu the logical conclusion to the policies begun by Gheorghiu-Dej on the eve of Stalin's death and accelerated after the removal of Soviet troops has been reached. Coincidentally (but unofficially) the problems of bureaucratization, so closely identified in Romanian discussions with the prewar rule of the bourgeoisie, have also resurfaced. To understand this problem, and the dilemmas it has posed for the regime, requires an understanding of the basic institutions of the current Romanian state.

PUBLIC ORGANIZATIONS IN SOCIALIST SOCIETY

In accordance with the socialist model dominant in Eastern Europe, there are three classes of public organizations in Romania: those belonging to the party, those identified with the state, and mass organizations designed to mobilize the entire population. All three follow the ideal of hierarchical organizations, strictly controlled from the top, under the principle of democratic centralism.

The Party and Institutionalized Personalism

As a vanguard and leadership organization, the party permeates all aspects of state and society. Operating through a three-tiered system of first secretaries, secretaries, and political executive committee members (consisting of members of the permanent bureau and regular committee members), Nicolae Ceaușescu stands supreme as head of the party and president of state. At the national level, besides Ceaușescu, the leadership structure of the party consists of eleven secretaries, nine members of the permanent bureau of the political executive committee, twenty-three political executive committee members, and fifteen candidate members. Within these components of the Central Committee (the composite term for all these roles) there are several interlocking positions—most notably that of Nicolae Ceauşescu himself, who is secretary general and member of the permanent bureau; his wife Elena, who is also a permanent bureau member as well as a regular member of the political executive committee; Iosif Uglar and Ilie Verdet, who are both secretaries and members of the political executive committee. Verdet is also a member of the permanent bureau of the political executive committee and Uglar holds a key government post equivalent to cabinet minister. While the Central Committee as a whole is officially the party's basic decision-making unit and is charged with selection of the nine-member permanent bureau, in effect it is the permanent bureau that is the primary power center. In his role as first party secretary, Ceauşescu prepares an annual party report, which is widely distributed and reported on at annual meetings. However, the major party assembly is the convocation of a full party congress every four years.

As is the case in all the other Eastern European regimes (with the exception of the rotation of executive leadership in Yugoslavia since Tito's death), the key figure in Romanian politics and government is the party's first secretary. Under Ceauşescu the cult of the leader and of personality has achieved new heights. It is this element that has been the object of considerable criticism within socialist circles in Romania and outside the country. Thus, when the charge of Stalinism is leveled at the regime by the party faithful, they are focusing attention on the cult of personality combined with the manipulation of power designed to insure the continued preeminence of a single individual.

The legal foundation for this emphasis on individual leadership can be found in Law No. 20/1969. Under this law the principle of collective leadership was abolished for the Council of Ministers, executive committees of all local organs of government, and ministers and other organs of state administration. In contrast, in economic organizations and state enterprises the principle of collective leadership was maintained. But while workers may exercise formal collective control, in effect leadership is provided by the plant manager appointed by the ministry responsible for the enterprise. An important corollary to the current individual leadership principle is the practice of assigning major party and key government roles to the same individuals. Just as Ceauşescu is both first party secretary and head of state, so too there is a fusion of executive leadership at the *judeţe* and local levels. In each instance the appropriate party first secretary is also president of the people's council and charged with policymaking responsibilities for that unit of government.

Nevertheless, to understand patterns of political power in contemporary Romania one must go one step further and look at family ties at the top. Here one encounters not only the all-pervasive presence of Nicolae Ceauşescu as head of state, first party secretary, and president of the state council, but that of other members of his family in equally visible and crucial political roles. Presently, the Ceauşescu family has become virtually a ruling dynasty. Besides the concentration of all major leadership roles in the person of Nicolae Ceauşescu, his wife Elena is one of three first deputy prime ministers, in addition to her positions mentioned above in the discussion of the Central Committee. Many attribute extensive power to her in the selection of cabinet lists for approval by her husband, much like the power wielded decades ago by Evita Peron in Argentina. Their son, Nicolae, is a secretary of the Romanian parliament, a candidate member of the party's Central Committee, and a former Communist party youth leader. The president's brother-in-law, Vasile Barbulescu, is a full member of the Central Committee; his wife's brother, Gheorghe Petrescu, is both a member of the Central Committee and a cabinet minister. Two of the president's brothers likewise hold important government posts: Ion Ceauşescu is deputy minister of agriculture and holds a key party position, while Ilie Ceauşescu holds the rank of major general in the Romanian army and occupies a senior post in the army's political council.[7] So extensive has the influence of Ceauşescu and his family become that is impossible to separate their personalities from the regime and the party.

State Institutions

Paralleling and interlocked with the party are institutions of the state similar to those of parliamentary government. Under the terms of the current constitution (1965),[8] the primary state institution is the Grand National Assembly, a unicameral body that is elected every five years and has one representative for each 40,000 inhabitants. Since 1965 it has consisted of 465 deputies, the majority of whom are classified as working class.[9] In 1965, for example, 47 percent were workers, 11.5 percent were peasants, and 41.5 percent were intellectuals.[10] Second only to the Grand National Assembly are the Council of State and the Presidency of the Republic. The Council of State is a twenty-two–member permanent legislative body with four vice presidents, elected by the National Assembly from among its membership for five-year terms. Charged with responsibility for establishing all assembly elections and making all appointments for central administrative organizations (except those of the

Council of Ministers), its head is the president of the republic. In this context the Presidency of the Republic is largely a staff organization immediately at the service of Ceauşescu in his role as head of state. Subordinate to the Council of State is the Council of Ministers, whose head is the prime minister. Elected by the assembly, it is principally a policymaking and policy-implementing body, directing state administration and routine, day-to-day governmental operations. It is charged specifically with responsibility for coordinating and overseeing ministerial activities, other central governmental organs (various executive committees and special councils), and state enterprises.[11]

One of the practices in state administration that is frequently confusing to the outsider is the principle of double subordination and the consequent status given to many public organizations as organs of state and party. Common to all Marxist-Leninist systems, this principle of double subordination has been carried in Romania to an extent unknown in other republics. This meshing of state and party organs occurs at all levels of government, from the Council of State (which was transformed by law in 1969 into a organ of the party and the state) down to the local level, where double subordination becomes a device for linking technical services provided by the central ministries to executive supervision and control by local people's council officials (who also are ranking local party personnel). The consequence of these multiple devices for coordinating and controlling state activities through hierarchical principles and the insurance of direct party supervision is a bewildering maze of committees, state councils, and independent administrative units outside the lines of authority provided by the central ministries. While the phenomenon of autonomous and semiautonomous state entities so common in the capitalist world does not appear in socialist society, an equally great coordination problem is presented by these tiers of authorities and coordinating committees set up for nearly every area of state life.

Corresponding to this hierarchy of public organizations is a hierarchy of laws paralleling that which has developed in the civil law countries of Western Europe. As a matter of fact, despite the separate status given to socialist law and the emphasis on new socialist reality, the foundation of the Romanian legal system and the application given to policy is heavily influenced by the civil law tradition common to Continental European states. Paralleling the above categorization of governmental institutions are assembly laws, state council decrees and legal decisions, and presidential decrees and legal decisions. Public finance follows an equally carefully demarked legalistic approach: the most comprehensive documents are the state plans (five-year and one-year); in descending order are the state budget, enabling legislation at the national level, and corresponding subordinate financial documents at the *judeţe* level.

Mass Organizations

The third institutional component of Romania as a socialist republic is the structure developed for coordinating and directing mass organizations (*organizaţiile obşteşti*): the Socialist Unity front (Frontul Unitaţii Socialiste, FUS). FUS is a political organization within which the Romanian Communist party exercises a leadership role. Its purpose is to mobilize the population through mass organizations set up on a corporate basis: the General Union of Labor Unions (Uniunea Generală a Sindicatelor din România), the National Union of Agricultural Cooperatives (Uniunea Naţională a Cooperativelor Agricole de Producţie), the Union of Communist Youth (Uniunea Tineretului Comunist), the National Women's Council (Consiliul Naţional a Femeilor), the Writers' Union (Uniunea Scritorilor), and similar organizations designed to embrace all other interests in Romanian society.

Present throughout society down to the village level, the primary activities of FUS are organizing electoral campaigns and fielding candidates for the National Assembly and the people's councils (regional and local governmental institutions).[12] From the standpoint of the overall functioning of Romanian politics and government, the most interesting aspect of FUS is not so much its electoral role as a single-party mass-movement organization; rather, it is the degree to which it measures up to the ideals and standards of state corporatism, as articulated and developed by Mihail Manoilescu in the prewar era.[13] The logical conclusion to the organization by the state of interest group associations, their grouping together in unions and councils, and the subsequent overarching national organization provided by FUS, with its preparation of the slate of candidates for the National Assembly, consequently has been reached under neither capitalism nor fascism but under state socialism.

SUBNATIONAL GOVERNMENT

The most extensive readjustments of Romanian governmental institutions, under Ceauşescu and in accordance with the country's status as a socialist republic since 1965, have occurred at the subnational level. Under current arrangements people's councils (*consilii populare*) operate at all subordinate levels of government, provincial as well as local. Here the fusion of political and administrative activities is the greatest.

Whereas at the national level a distinction is maintained between political or representative institutions and administrative ones, the people's councils are simultaneously organs for representation and administration. Giving further weight to this fusion of powers at the subnational level is the fact that it is commonplace for the party to be housed in the same building, with separate entrances maintained for party activities as opposed to state-administration-related ones. As ranking provincial party people are frequently also members of the people's councils' executive comittees, communication between these two sets of offices is facilitated.

Provincial Government

Management functions and responsibility for program administration are housed in the executive committee under the direction of a first secretary, a first vice president (in larger localities), and one to five vice presidents.[14] Within the offices assigned to the executive committee are also located what are known as local specialized organs for state administration (*organele locale de specialitate ale administrație de stat*): finance, agriculture, commerce, education, health, etc. These organs function according to the above-mentioned criterion of double subordination, whereby their employees (who are considered to be local and not national civil servants) are accountable to the local political leadership (the executive committee) and the local people's council, as well as to their corresponding parallel central ministerial organization.[15] Besides these administrative services, which are provided through executive committees, *judeţe* organizations have additional responsibilities. Including the above category these are four: administrative offices and bureaus (*direcţii şi birouri*), central organs of control (*corpuri de control*), the provincial inspectorate (*inspectorate*), and administrative services for localities subordinated to the provincial people's council.[16]

Administrative services provided by the provincial people's councils are made further complex by the practice of distinguishing between specialized administrative services (*organele locale de specialitate ale administrație de stat*) and the executive committee's own administrative apparatus (*aparatul propriu*). Belonging to the latter category are offices for local state administration such as legal services and civil records (Direcţia pentru administraţia locală de stat); planning and wages (Direcţia planificare şi salarizare); investments (Direcţia tehnică investiţii); urban planning, architecture, and construction control (Direcţia sistematizare, arhitectură şi control construcţii); the people's council president's own control corps (Corpul de control al preşedintelui); state commerce (Inspectoratul comercial de stat); prices (Oficiul de preţuri şi tarife); spas and tourist services (Serviciul balneo-climatic şi turistic); secretarial and staff services (Serviciul secretariat-administrativ). In the former one finds six services: a directorate-general for agriculture, agro-industry, food, forestry, and mineral water (Direcţia generală pentru agricultură, industrie alimentară, silvicultură şi ape), a directorate for commercial activities (Direcţia comercială), an inspectorate for schools (Inspectoratul judeţean şcolar), a directorate for worker problems and social services (Direcţia pentru problemele muncii şi ocrotirii sociale), health services (Direcţia sanitară), and a committee for culture and art (Comitetul pentru cultură şi artă).[17] The basic division between these two kinds of services is twofold: whether the services are related to the national plan (the latter) or the local plan (the former) and the degree of double subordination encountered (formal double accountability exists only in the latter category, although in the former—where technical advice, personnel, and services not available within the province are needed—recourse to the central government does take place. Insofar as record-keeping is concerned, only those people specifically assigned as technical personnel and those on leave from a central ministry (either short-term or long-term) are considered to be civil servants. The thousands of local-level employees engaged in the provision of administrative services are not officially recorded and thus it is possible to maintain a relatively low figure when reporting the number of state bureaucrats.

Local Government Controls

Apart from these administrative operations and the practice of distinguishing between local- and national-plan-related activities, it is interesting to note the attention devoted to control and supervision of local affairs. These fall into the other three categories spelled out in the jurisdiction of the provincial council: control organs (essentially legalistic and financial in character), the provincial inspectorate (consisting of agents belonging to the provincial office who are sent out to "visit" local people's councils and deal with problems arising within them), and the coordination of administrative services provided at the local level. Insofar as the actual operation of government is concerned, the double set of controls and three well-defined and hierarchically structured levels of government have produced an administrative apparatus that is highly centralized—one in which there are many different levels of clearance that must be gone through before concrete actions can take place, and one in which extreme caution is exercised to make certain that the necessary approval of higher-ups has been obtained and that the local agent authorizing the activity will not be penalized for an action he should not have permitted to be executed.

Program Autonomy

There are, however, two areas of economic activity where the rigid controls resulting from this administrative system are minimized or at least less severe: agriculture and industry. While the principle of double subordination applies to agriculture as it does to other services, agriculture enjoys a great deal more program autonomy. Accordingly, it is common to find the provincial office for agricultural affairs housed separately from the local people's council. In each *judeţe* there is a directorate-general for agricultural affairs, subordinate to the Ministry of Agriculture and to the provincial people's council.

In industry, there is even greater autonomy, as only those industries categorized as local fall directly under the jurisdiction of the provincial people's council. All major industries and plants are categorized as republican industries and fall under the jurisdiction of one of the country's central economic ministries. It is only through party activities that there is intervention at the provincial level in the operations of these economic organizations. The people's councils have no jurisdiction in this area at all. Once again, though—to illustrate the overall emphasis placed on central planning and controls—it is the National Council for the People's Councils (Consiliul pentre probelemele consiliilor populare, CPCP) that is charged with responsibility for supervising activities specifically within the province of the people's councils (those activities specifically assigned to the councils under the category of *aparatul propriu*). Overall coordination, of course, of all economic activities occurs through the State Planning Committee (Comitetul de stat al planificarii), and economic controls come from the Finance Ministry (Ministerul finanţilor).

Representative Functions

Finally, in assessing the activities of the people's councils, it is important to call attention to the emphasis Romanian sources place on their representative function. The laws regulating these aspects go into considerable detail to spell out the number of representatives according to the subnational unit of governance concerned.[18] Some idea of the overall basis of representation can be gained by looking at 1973 statistics on the breakdown of deputies to the people's councils. Of the 136,932 deputies serving in people's councils at the commune level, 84 percent were peasants, 8 percent were workers, and 8 percent were intellectuals. At the provincial level, of the 7,818 deputies serving, 50 percent were workers, 30 percent were intellectuals, and 20 percent were peasants.[19] Nevertheless, when one examines the actual activities of the people's councils the representative function is clearly second to the administrative function of providing public services and regulating various aspects of life at the subnational level. The day-to-day operations of the people's councils are bureaucratic ones, directed by members of the executive committee of the people's councils and executed by staff employees. The image thus is one of a mass-movement, mobilization system; the reality is a bureaucratic polity in which the bureaucrat reigns supreme and citizens are clearly in a subordinate position from which they must negotiate, request, and beseech the action of government officials for this or that permit. State controls exist in multiple form and affect nearly every phase of day-to-day life.

MANAGEMENT ISSUES IN A DEVELOPING SOCIALIST ECONOMY

Not surprisingly, as the regime has become institutionalized, bureaucratic problems have resurfaced. If, on the one hand, the revolutionary breakthrough experienced by Romania after World War II radically reshaped national society, on the other hand, one does encounter continuity between pre- and postwar Romania in the presence of a highly centralized state and the longstanding practice of dealing with the bulk of the population as subjects, as unequal participants in a society where numerous services must be extracted from government bureaucrats representing and interpreting the intent of the state. If anything, the range of services provided by the state has increased under socialism, as has recourse to the state for resolution of social necessities. In contemporary Romania there remain few areas in national life outside the purview of government. The modern Romanian state, accordingly, consists of hundreds, if not thousands, of public organizations, operating at all levels of society in hierarchical and parallel relationships.

Improving Performance

In this context, improving the quality of public management has become a concern of the party. Although Gheorghiu-Dej called attention to the problems of bureaucratism as early as 1960, specific action dates from a 1966 decision of the Central Committee to sponsor work of a managerial nature. This was followed by a public statement at the December 1967 National Conference of the Romanian Communist party regarding the need to incorporate modern concepts and methods of organization in the management of state enterprises. Since that time considerable experimentation, research, writing, and training have gone on in Romania in the field defined as "scientific organization."[20]

As a consequence of this concern with performance in state enterprises and in other development-related programs, the Central Committee authorized in 1967 the creation of a public management training center within the party's Academy Ştefan Gheorghiu: the Center for the Preparation of Leadership Cadres in State Enterprises (Centrul de perfecționare [a pregătirii] cadrelor de conducere din întreprinderi, CEPECA). Beginning as a program for training managerial personnel engaged in factory operations, by the 1970s it had been expanded to include civil servants, trained in law, pursuing careers in state administration. Such men usually began their careers as district inspectors; as they proceeded up the "control" hierarchy to the rank of provincial secretary (secretar), it was recognized that their responsibility for overseeing development-related programs increased. Hence, improving their skills in areas defined as "direct administration" also has become a priority.[21]

Accompanying this authorization was the institution of counterpart operations at various levels of government: the creation of cadres for the resolution of organizational problems involving production and labor, the formation in fifty-six of the country's largest cities of cabinets devoted to problems of scientific organization in production and work, the organization of a training institute in the Ministry of Labor (Institutul de conducere şi organizare a producției), the creation of offices for organization and control in the central ministries, the authorization of additional executive training programs in other state sectors, and the development of national guidelines for state enterprises. The culmination of this whole movement was the establishment in 1973 of a national council to coordinate and attend to these needs on a national basis: the Council for Organizational Problems of a Socio-Economic Nature (Consiliu pentru problemele organizarii economic-sociale).[22]

Despite these auspicious beginnings, by the end of the 1970s official support for what had become a Romanian version of the scientific management movement had waned. The charge was that those identified with this new field too often were unable to demonstrate a notable improvement in the quality of operations in areas of immediate concern to the party's top leadership. Nevertheless, CEPECA has continued in its role as a training center and is today the most important such operation in the country. Its impact on public organizations, extending now over a period of more than a decade, has gradually expanded until its charge has come to include all key management personnel in the country. Operating under a 1971 decision (hotarirea) of the Central Committee, its responsibilities currently include the training of leadership cadres for the party, state administration, and mass organizations where management problems involving socioeconomic activities are encountered. As a consequence of this blanket authorization and commitment to upgrading the quality of public management, and despite attacks on individual academics, CEPECA trained 16,000 cadre personnel in a variety of short- and long-term courses between 1967 and 1973.[23]

Public Management Materials

Throughout the 1970s a considerable literature developed as a counterpart to this interest in training managerial personnel. Even though its intellectual origins were clearly based on Western business administration materials, especially those developed in the United States, emphasis in the Romanian context was placed on the adjustment of scientific management techniques to fit the needs of socialist society. These were twofold: assurance that the techniques advocated were compatible with Marxist-Leninist principles and the utilization of a terminology more appropriate for the Romanian context. The former was accomplished by including lengthy statements at the beginning of each of the major texts, summarizing relevant Marxist-Leninist principles and showing how they supported the concern with greater economy, efficiency, and rationality in management. The basic adjustment, in the eyes of these authors, was to make the techniques designed for private business fit the needs of public enterprise. The latter was accomplished by designating the "new science" as a "management science for socialist society" ("ştiinţa conducerii societăţii socialiste").

Summing up this whole perspective is the introductory statement prepared by Miron Constantinescu, one of the party's more cosmopolitan members, for one of the primary texts developed to introduce this material.

> The conscience construction of socialist society, in order not to become subjected to spontaneous or random action, presupposes the maintenance of management activities in social life by the party of the working class, based on prior [knowledge or] mastery of the management sciences. A management science adequate for social life must be capable of directing political action in accord with the principles of scientific management, concrete methods, and techniques of sociopolitical management; these constitute the methodology of social management. The most important aspect of these principles, methods, and specific techniques for managing socialist society is their recognition of the decision as the most important unit in management.[24]

Complementing this body of literature, much of which is closely affiliated with the activities of centers of economic research and training, has been the development of a field in the country's law programs known as "scientific state administration." Incorporating older legalistic perspectives in training people for public law careers and employment by the state, the administrative sciences as taught in the law schools and other legal training centers emphasize the need to master traditional public law materials as well as the newer techniques of scientific management. Both before and since the transition to socialism there has been a need in Romanian public administration for persons trained in public law. This is because the predominant approach to policy implementation remains legalistic and the foundation of socialist law, as practiced in Romania, continues to be a civil law system in tune with Continental jurisprudence. As in other civil law systems, there is an elaborate hierarchy of laws, decrees, and decisions that are legally binding and subsequent detailed legislation regulating their implementation. In addition, the controls identified with centralized economic planning and careful regulation of all aspects of national life are applied in a legalistic fashion. As a consequence, in postwar as well as prewar Romania the role of the *secretar* at various levels of government has been crucial. Whether serving in a small town, a municipality (that is, a city or town that has received the designation of *municipiu*, a governmental category common to other southern European and Latin American political systems influenced by Roman law traditions), a major city, or a provincial capital, he is a person, trained in law, who is charged with the administration of day-to-day affairs and is responsible for the interpretation of legal documents transferred down from superior governmental levels.

Training Provincial Authorities

Recognizing the important role played by the *secretar*, when experimentation began with new forms of training for party, state, and mass organization personnel charged with leadership responsibilities, specific programs were also developed for those specializing in state administration, specifically those filling the role of *secretar* (or, at an intermediate level, *inspector*). Thus, a substantial part of scientific management materials published in Romania during the 1970s has been by specialists in public law engaged in training students for state administration careers and aware of the need to prepare these students in a way different from the past. Likewise, there are both intermediate programs, such as the one in Sibiu, where the student does not receive a full law degree but is prepared to occupy intermediate positions in the provincial administration, and various short-term training courses for mid-career personnel either at the Ştefan Gheorghiu Academy (the most prestigious) or within the larger *judeţe,* such as Iaşi, where specific courses of this type have been taught for a number of years. Again, following the Continental European practice of early career selection, there are several specialized secondary schools in the country for persons wishing to pursue a state administration career, viz the *liceu* in Iaşi set up for the purpose of training people for the provincial inspectorate.

Both in the university-level courses and the mid-career courses, there is specific training in present administrative practice in Romania (with the use of organizational charts and other aids) as well as the study of and lectures from scientific administration materials, in the tradition of the scientific management movement. Technique is a substantial part of this teaching and the result is not unlike what I, as a researcher, discovered fifteen years ago working with training programs in Brazil, another administrative system heavily influenced by Continental civil law traditions: a revitalized juridical perspective combined with the interpretation of scientific management principles, norms, and techniques designed to produce a technocratic model of administration – one that emphasizes economy, efficiency, rationality, and nonpolitical approaches to governmental problems and issues.[25] When one speaks of the problems of bureaucratism in contemporary Romania it thus becomes important not only to understand the rigidities that have developed as a consequence of socialist practice – especially the emphasis on democratic centralism – but also the older governmental patterns present in the country: personalism (the excessive concentration of executive power in the hands of a single individual and his close associates) and legalism (the conceptualization of government not as a dynamic process of accommodation and negotiation among diverse interests, but essentially as administration, i.e., the application and interpretation of public laws designed to regulate and provide for as wide a range of social life as possible).

CONCLUSIONS

The rekindling of nationalism under socialism in Romania consequently has several facets: the consolidation of ethnic Romanian leadership over the PCR and its conversion into a mass-mobilization organization providing the leadership for the Socialist Unity front, the institutionalization of the regime, and the development of a strong national state capable of serving effectively as the sole mediator between external actors and citizens of the state. The changes identified with this process of consolidating the new socialist order have entailed moving beyond the establishment of a "revolutionary breakthrough" toward rule by a new governing elite untainted by experience and knowledge of prewar Romania, except as taught in the schools and provided for in official propaganda designed to reinforce Romanian nationalism. These years span the governments of Gheorghiu-Dej and Ceauşescu. While initiated by Gheorghiu-Dej, this rekindling of nationalism under socialism has become identified especially with the Ceauşescu regime. The late 1960s and the 1970s marked the era of greatest realization of these goals and programs. Much was accomplished during these years in terms of economic growth, population relocation into urban centers, and the creation of grass-roots organizations.

The problem is that by 1980 these changes had become so closely identified with the personality of Nicolae Ceauşescu that it was impossible to separate the two. Romania's negotiated autonomy hence is limited by a kind of Marxist-Leninist orthodoxy that has produced a regime that is quite conservative in its actions. While publicly defying the Soviet Union from time to time on various policy issues (such as the fall 1979 refusal to participate in Warsaw Pact military maneuvers), it has never been subjected to the charge of deviationism and the prospect of direct Soviet intervention to "purify" the party leadership.

There is no doubt at the moment of Ceauşescu's supremacy in Romania. His position as the head of state and party first secretary is currently unchallenged. But the concentration of all power in Ceauşescu's hands and continued action to insure that predominance (such as the continuous rotation of persons into and out of top government and party leadership roles) has led to the creation of tremendous bottlenecks in day-to-day government. The governmental process today in Romania is above all a hierarchical system in which orders and inputs flow downward and upward through a well-established set of procedures. The problem is that, while routine aspects of government can be expedited fairly effectively when the demand is made, delays, excessive caution, and unwillingness to take action without assurance of approval by superiors are readily observable. Nevertheless, the system operates most effectively when orders are issued at the top and compliance is expected from below. In contrast, the individual citizen has little leverage under these conditions. Requests for governmental services require considerable effort—willingness to pursue solutions to individual needs through repeated effort, extensive paper formalities, and waiting frequently in line as one passes from one governmental office to another.

As a consequence of these developments, governmental action has become predominantly bureaucratic, in that the majority of the state's activities are regulated and interpreted by government bureaucrats. The party is certainly all-pervasive and Marxist-Leninist ideology continually projected before the public. But the party remains essentially a vanguard organization providing leadership, making decisions for the country as a whole, and mobilizing the citizenry as needed. It delegates to state bureaucrats responsibility for day-to-day operations.

By 1980 the dynamism that characterized the late 1960s had clearly come to an end. While official statistics continued to show sustained economic growth – as a part of necessary official party policy – most external analysts had begun to call attention to a slowing down of the rate of economic growth. Romania has exhausted the "easy" areas for industrial development – those activities that would parallel under socialism the playing out of the possibilities of import-export substitution and the establishment of basic industries in mixed-economy, middle-range developing countries. Concurrent with this slowing down of economic growth Romania is facing a number of other problems parallel to difficulties encountered by countries outside the socialist bloc: labor unrest; rising costs for basic necessities (housing, food, urban services, transportation); an energy crisis. There are also difficulties identified with rigidities within the state apparatus and the lack of flexibility in creating new responses, as a consequence of multiple decision-making centers, and control and coordination dilemmas.

Yet problems such as these should not be interpreted to suggest a weakening of the Ceauşescu regime. If anything, Ceauşescu's control is more secure now than at any time in the past and his power virtually unchallenged. The immediate prognosis, then, is not continued pressure for change and new responses to the pressures underway, but increased authoritarianism as the authority of the state is used to reinforce personal power and rule.

Each of the ingredients touched on in this chapter, while a separate topic in itself, is part of the overall picture presented by national communism. A particular set of political events marks the transition to socialism in Romania. To an understanding of these must be added an awareness of the public organizations through which rule by the PCR is maintained and how the organizations are used to regulate social life in a complex society. This situation created concern with management issues as topics of sufficient import to require continuous attention and periodic public statements by the party leadership. It is interesting to note in this regard that greater effectiveness in the administration of development programs and in the ability of the state to regulate conflict in national society have become as important a set of priorities under socialism as they have become in mixed-economy, middle-range developing countries. This requires a reassessment of the facile interpretations given by dependency theorists in the West to the differences between capitalism and socialism. The transition to socialism does not necessarily presume an easy resolution to the dilemmas of development, but rather their reappearance in another form.

With the background of this institutional setting, we can proceed to a discussion of Romania's internal development policies and external foreign policy perspectives.

NOTES

1. Stephen Fischer-Galati, *The New Romania: From People's Republic to Socialist Republic* (Cambridge: MIT Press, 1967), p. 79, and Arhiva CC al PCR, fondul 1, dosarul 9, fila 95, dosarul 235, fila 1, as cited in Ştefan Lache, "Activitatea Partidului Comunist Român pentru democratizarea aparatului de stat în perioada marţie 1945–decembrie 1947" [The work of the Romanian Communist party in the democratization of the state apparatus for the period March 1945–December 1947] (Bucureşti: Teză de doctorat, Academia de Invăţămant Social-Politic "Ştefan Gheorghiu" de pe lîngă CC al PCR, Facultatea de filozofie-istorie, 1970), p. 418. Fischer-Galati's actual phrase is "less than 600,000 with a further increase to 'nearly 850,000'" by 1960. Of these he estimates 150,000 were activists.

2. Lache, p. 418.

3. COMECON is the acronym for the Eastern bloc's common market arrangement, first set up by the Soviet Union in 1949 as the Council for Mutual Economic Assistance. From the Romanian perspective COMECON has always functioned as a Soviet vehicle for forcing on it unwanted economic politics.

4. Published in Bucharest by Meridiane in 1967, as the "Report delivered by Ceauşescu at the National Conference of the Romanian Communist Party, December 6, 1967" (English-language version).

5. Nicolae Ceauşescu, "1967 Report," p. 133.

6. Ceauşescu, "1967 Report," pp. 121, 23, 25.

7. Eric Bourne, "Romania's Ruling Dynasty Expands," *Christian Science Monitor* (April 1, 1980), p. 7.

8. Since 1944 Romania has had three constitutions: 1948 (regulating the transition to socialism), 1952 (setting up institutions corresponding to a Soviet-style people's republic), and 1965 (adjusting existing institutions in accord with Romania's self-declared status as an autonomous socialist republic).

9. Tudor Drăganu and Tudor O. Gradea, "Perfecţionarea formelor şi metodelor de asigurare a legalităţii în administraţia de stat" [The improvement of the forms and methods (used) to assure legality in state administration] (pamphlet) (Bucureşti: Asociaţia Juriştilor din R.S.R., 1971), pp. 7–8.

10. Ian M. Matley, *Romania: A Profile* (New York: Praeger, 1970), p. 144.

11. Tudor Drăganu, *Drept constituţional* [Constitutional law] (Bucureşti: Editura didactică şi pedagogică, 1972), pp. 390–393.

12. Ioan Ceterchi (ed.), *Organizațiile obștești în sistemul organizării politice din Republica Socialistă România* [Mass organizations in the system of political organizations in the Socialist Republic of Romania] (București: Editura academiei republicii socialiste România, 1973), pp. 63–65, 73.

13. Mihail Manoilescu, *Le siècle du corporatisme* [The century of corporatism] (Paris: F. Alcan, 1934). For a summary of Manoilescu's ideas – both as a statement of his political thought and as a primary source for understanding corporatist theory – see Philippe C. Schmitter, "Reflections on Mihail Manoilescu and the Political Consequences of Delayed-Dependent Development on the Periphery of Western Europe," in Kenneth Jowitt (ed.), *Social Change in Romania, 1860–1940: A Debate on Development in a European Nation,* Research Series No. 36 (Berkeley: Institute of International Studies, University of California, 1978), pp. 117–130.

14. At the *judeţe* level there is a president, a first vice president and three vice presidents, of whom two must be secretaries within the *judeţ* party organization. While the *judeţe* of Covasna, Harghiţa, Ialomiţa, Satu Mare, Salaj, Tulcea, and Vrancea have executive committees of fifteen (including the foregoing leadership roles), all other *judeţe* executive committees have seventeen members. The Bucharest executive committee has, however, nineteen members and five vice presidents instead of three. All other local councils have executive committees with nine members (in localities up to 80,000 inhabitants), eleven (in those over 80,000 but under 120,000) and twelve in centers over 120,000. Except for the latter category, these councils all have two vice presidents; cities over 120,000 have three. Again, within this top leadership two must also be party secretaries in the local party organization. For further details and verification, see România, *Legislaţie,* "Legea 57/1968 de organizare şi funcţionare a consiliilor populare; Legea 5/1975 privind congresul camera legislativă şi conferinţele consiliilor populare; Decretul Consiliului de Stat 21/1975 cu privire la compunerea comitetelor şi a birourile executive ale consiliilor populare" [*Legislation:* Law no. 57/1968 for the organization and functioning of the People's Councils; Law no. 5/1975 concerning the Congressional Legislative Chamber and Conferences of the People's Councils; Council of State Decree No. 21/1975 concerning the composition of the committees and the executive bureaus of the People's Councils] (pamphlet) (București: Consiliul de stat, 1976), 40 pp.

15. Ceterchi, p. 54.

16. Nicolae Anghel, Ion Cocoli, Alexandru Negoiţa, and Nicolae Radu, *Conducerea şi organizarea administraţiei şi economie locale: conducerea şi organizarea administraţiei locale – manuel pentru liceu de specialitate, anul III* [Management and the organization of administration and the local economy: the management and organization of local administration – a manual for specialized lycées, third year] (București: Editura didactică şi pedagogică, 1971), p. 94.

17. Anghel, pp. 94–95, 110–111.

18. The basic law here is Law No. 57/1968, although it is Law No. 2/1968 that sets out the overall organization of subnational government since 1968.

19. Ioan Vida, *Deputatul, împuternicit şi factor mobilizator al cetăţenilor* [The

deputy as representative and element for mobilizing the citizenry] (Bucureşti: Editura politică, 1973), p. 8.

20. Ovidiu Nicolescu, *Perfecţionarea organizării conducerii intreprinderii (variable organizaţionale, analize, tehnici şi metode)* [The improvement of enterprise management organizations (organizational variables, analysis, techniques and methods)] (Bucureşti: Editura academiei republicii socialiste România, 1973), pp. 29–30.

21. Nicolescu, pp. 29–30.

22. *Formarea şi perfecţionarea cadrelor de conducere* [The formation and improvement of management cadres] (Bucureşti: Editura politică, 1971), p. x.

23. Nicolescu, p. 108.

24. Quote from the introduction written by Miron Constantinescu to *Introducere în ştiinţa conducerii societatii socialiste: studii şi cercetări de teren realizate de laboratorul de ştiinţa conducerii societăţi socialiste sub îndrumarea acad. prof. Miron Constantinescu* [Introduction to the scientific management of socialist societies: studies and field research as realized in the laboratory of scientific management for socialist societies under the direction of academician Professor Miron Constantinescu] (Bucureşti: Editura politică, 1974), a volume cosponsored by the Academia de ştiinţe sociale şi politice and the Academia Ştefan Gheorghiu, p. 11.

25. See Chapters 2 and 3 in my *Civil Service Reform in Brazil: Principles vs. Practice* (Austin: University of Texas Press, 1968). Romanian source materials that parallel this perspective and mentality and can be identified with scientific state administration are: Ilie Iovănas, *Dreptul administrativ şi elemente ale ştiinţei administraţie* [Administrative law and administrative science principles] (Bucureşti: Editura didactică şi pedagogică, 1977); Alexandru Negoiţă, *Stiinţa administraţiei* [Administrative science] (Bucureşti: Editura didactică şi pedagogică, 1977); Mihai T. Oroveanu, *Introducere în stiinţa administraţiei de stat* [Introduction to state administrative science] (Bucureşti: Editura enciclopedică romană, 1975); and Ioan Velea, *Conducătorul intreprinderii, specialist şi om politic* [The enterprise manager as specialist and political man] (Bucureşti: Editura politică, 1974). While the first three books are written by law professors and focus specifically on state administration, the latter exemplifies the genre developed in economic institutes and the like for persons pursuing careers as plant managers. Both meet in the common terrain established by acceptance of scientific management as the solution to bureaucratism in state organization.

4

Development: For Whom and For What?

No treatment of contemporary Romania can be considered complete without assessing the outcome of thirty years of concerted national planning stressing balanced economic growth as the solution to Romania's historic problem of underdevelopment. Concomitant with this emphasis on socioeconomic development has been transformation of the state bureaucracy and staffing of public positions with personnel capable of responding to the regime's demands for policies and programs designed to produce accelerated "multilateral development." Throughout Ceauşescu's rule, the phrase "multilateral development" has become a core aspect of the ideology of socialist construction, one subject to almost daily repetition and reminder. By this concept the regime means to convey to all concerned its goal of achieving full development of Romania's potential as a nation-state–industrially, commercially, and agriculturally. As a consequence public documents, news releases, and official publications make available on a yearly basis statistics demonstrating sustained economic growth and continual increases in productivity. The image projected thus is one of dynamism, of a regime always on the move and constantly engaged in employing the nation's economic and human resources to the fullest extent possible.

Given the primacy of the state as agent and executor of development policies and programs, the regime has long considered inculcation of state bureaucrats with the ideology of socialist construction and development an essential ingredient. As noted in Chapter 2, the first step was to remove state personnel identified with the old regime and to blanket in those committed to building a socialist society. Once the new regime was consolidated, party loyalty and socialist commitment were no longer sufficient; in addition it was recognized that there was an immediate need for new personnel with technical skills and specialized knowledge in fields linked to socioeconomic development. Accordingly, as described in Chapter 3, institutionalization of the regime and attention to development programs and policies led to the awareness that, in addition to specialized technical personnel, the state must have on hand more effective managers in all aspects of national life; hence, the interest in and cultivation of scientific-management research and training.

BUREAUCRATISM IN SOCIALIST SOCIETY

In the process of transforming the state into an apparatus dominated by the PCR and merging top leadership positions in state and party organs, new problems of bureaucratism have surfaced: excessive centralization of authority, rigidities in the interpretation of rules and regulations, lengthy delays in processing paperwork and formal requests, competing jurisdictions and overlapping responsibilities derived from the multiplicity of public organizations – some with parallel assignments of authority, others with ill-defined superior-subordinate relationships. Even though socialist administrative theorists like Lajos Szamel emphasize that, generically speaking, bureaucratic problems under state socialism are inherently different from those experienced by bourgeois capitalist states,[1] what is striking are the parallels encountered in the problems confronted by both kinds of states, especially those in the middle-range developing state category that have already made considerable progress in industrial and agricultural development but have yet to cross the threshold identifying them with the more advanced industrial economies.

The View from Below

Leaving aside comparison with other socialist and capitalist societies, what is most notable about the Romanian administrative system is how little the change in state forms – in the transition from capitalism to socialism – has affected the substance of administration when viewed from the standpoint of services to individual citizens. While it is difficult to measure these dimensions in concrete terms, the pervasiveness of red tape, the multiplicity of bureaucratic organizations charged with different responsibilities for the same areas, the need to do battle with countless numbers of government bureaucrats to obtain the most routine permissions and documents, the extensive regulations and controls imposed by the state over individual lives all suggest that the substance of the bureaucratic polity characterizing prewar Romania – administrative centralism, the unilateral imposition of central government policy, arbitrariness in state action, and stringent police control – has changed little. The major difference is the extensiveness of the contemporary state and the limited number of areas left to individual initiative.

To assess this dimension of bureaucracy requires focusing attention on the state from the vantage point of the average citizen, not that of the top leadership where aggregate indices of productivity are used. Yet, some immediate disclaimers must be made. Such a perspective does not argue that there is continuity per se between bureaucratic structures identified with the old regime and the new, for it would be a misreading of the revolutionary changes imposed after 1945 to develop such a theme. The ruptures in the previous state apparatus (between 1945 and 1950) and the new governmental system modeled after Soviet experience (implanted in 1950 and maintained without basic alterations until 1968) provided a place for a single political organization, the Romanian Communist party, and firmly established the principle of democratic centralism. Transferred into bureaucratic terms, these changes implied the fusion of state and party roles and the imposition of controls over bureaucratic actions that would insure compliance with party directives.

Continuities in Bureaucratic Behavior

What, then, are the sources of these continuities in administrative behavior if the context of revolutionary change in political, social, and economic structures is accepted as a given? Analysis of data collected from field research in Romania, based on 183 Romanian library sources and 110 interviews in Bucharest and throughout the country, suggests a nexus of relationships derived from excessive centralism. These involve continuity in the form of bureaucratic organization used, hierarchical concepts of authority that separate the governing elite from the masses, and the emphasis placed on control rather than service in public bureaucracy.

First, prewar and postwar Romania alike constitute instances where the concept of a unitary state has remained a fundamental premise. The continuation and expansion of this concept, whether under socialism or capitalism, necessitates reliance on public bureaucracy as the primary agent for regulation and development. This is perhaps to belabor the obvious, but it warrants repeating. The problems of bureaucratism — derived from the concentration of authority and control in the hands of bureaucrats, party as well as state — become all the more acute where the state and the economy are synonymous, where virtually all economic activity (except for such residual categories as individual ownership of small parcels of land in isolated rural areas or the marketing of religious candles by the church) falls within the public sector.

Second, the limited accounts available regarding bureaucratic performance in prewar and postwar Romania suggest an enormous dichotomy between state and society, if "society" is understood to mean the mass of the Romanian population. The bourgeois state, as it is called, was clearly at the service of a limited social class. Szamel calls attention to this fact as a part of the prewar reality common to all the central European states. Andrew Janos emphasizes the merger of the parliamentarian and bureaucratic systems under the constitutional monarchy in Romania and the pervasiveness of clientelism as the integrating mechanism before 1940. Stefan Zeletin documents the economic and political development of Romania in the 1920s in terms of its benefits to the new national bourgeoisie with a clarity and insightfulness that has yet to be surpassed.[2] But what is often overlooked in the evaluation of the current Romanian state is comparison between past and present and the relevancy of Milovan Djilas's critique of the Yugoslav state in the early 1950s.

The maintenance of the apparatus of the unitary state, the replacement of one class (the national bourgeoisie) with another (the Communist party elite), and change in the occupancy of bureaucratic roles without redefinition of their responsibilities has led to the perpetuation in large part of earlier patterns of political and administrative behavior and the entrance of a new elite that, after time has passed, has become subject to the same criticism made of the old.[3] Certainly there have been changes. State structures exist in far greater number than ever before as the state has assumed responsibility for regulating and stimulating all economic activity. The upper-class consumption patterns of the new elite are more frequently hidden from public view than were those of the old and are more likely to be disguised by the fact that the new currency of exchange is more often access to a limited number of luxury commodities and services than possession of monetary resources. Whereas administrative services in prewar Romania were concentrated in twelve mainline ministries, present-day Romania maintains thirty-six distinct central state organs charged with administrative responsibilities, the majority of which are engaged in economic activities of the most varied sort.[4]

Third, the emphasis placed on control rather than service in public bureaucracy is tied closely to centralism and hierarchical organization. In the context of a command economy with a centralized planning apparatus and well-established hierarchical relations within major organizations, policy orders and changes can move upward and downward throughout the public bureaucracy with a good deal of efficiency and effectiveness. This is especially the case with policy changes decreed at the top. On the other hand, many routine matters initiated at the local level through district and provincial people's councils take an inordinate amount of time to resolve – especially when they require departure from the plan for a given year; these almost always require referral to

Bucharest. An elaborate planning apparatus does exist, which emphasizes popular consultation and participation at all levels, but it is largely formalistic in its operation, with the effective and real decisions being made quite clearly at the center. Aside from the great emphasis placed on plan coordination and the integration of party and state organs at provincial and district levels, from the standpoint of the individual citizen, administrative services such as authorization to change one's dwelling, permission to move from one area of the country to another, requests for specialized medical attention in a clinic other than the one to which a person has been assigned, and the processing of school papers require extensive and involved relations with public bureaucracy.

While individual experiences do not necessarily prove the case, perhaps a number of examples taken from a personal log kept of encounters with state administration over a twelve-month period (September 1977 through August 1978) will illustrate these points more effectively. During this time my family and I lived within the context of the local economy and without many of the advantages usually given to foreign visitors. It took five months (September 15–February 22) to work out an accommodation on housing (without ever actually getting into an apartment), four months (September 15–January 13) to arrange approval through the Ministry of Education to enroll one of my children in a music *liceu* (*lycée*) on a part-time basis, five months (November 11–April 11) to work out approval within party and state organs to undertake fieldwork. This request for authorization to travel freely through the countryside had been discussed during a preliminary visit six months prior to undertaking the long-term visit, had been listed on my official papers, and – in terms of a specific itinerary – had been approved prior to arrival. Another example is the five working days I spent in lines and various government offices to register a car and obtain a title transfer from the seller (a departing foreigner). While Szamel discusses the problem of red tape under democratic centralism in the abstract and attempts to separate it from bourgeois centralism, the daily life of most nationals entails extensive and intensive involvement with different facets of state bureaucracy. Looking at the state from the grass roots level, one is continuously confronted with a bewildering array of regulations and government offices, each with its own organizational identity and distinctive set of procedures and operations.

CIVIL SERVICE TRAINING AND SOCIALIZATION

How are civil servants trained before and after entry into government service? My data suggest that normal entry into civil service careers continues to be through one of the country's three main law

schools in Bucharest, Iaşi, and Cluj-Napoca. There is also a relatively
new program in the Faculty of Economic and Administrative Law in
Sibiu, begun in 1971, to train people for careers in the provincial
bureaucracy. Exceptions to this generalization fall into two categories:
the filling of more specialized bureaucratic positions – where professional training in education, medicine, economics, architecture, and
engineering are the norm – and the hiring of plant managers. Despite
these patterns, which can be identified with the new professionalism encountered elsewhere in the contemporary world and most likely to appear where social and economic development programs are underway,
the world of the Romanian bureaucrat remains heavily legalistic.

Legalism under Socialism

Bureaucratic procedures and operations follow a carefully prescribed set of laws and regulations; the concern with the legality of each
action is great; and the general orientation is one that is very much in
tune with the civil law traditions of Continental Europe. Certainly the
category known as socialist law entails legal principles and concepts at
variance with civil practices in Western Europe, but the difference is
more one of style than of content. The concern with codes, the extensive
listings of various categories of decree law and laws passed by the Grand
National Assembly, and the great attention given to administrative law
as the proper way to handle questions and procedures in public administration suggest considerable continuity between past and present
when one looks at performance. Granted, there are marked generational
differences between prewar civil servants and contemporary bureaucrats, but I would suggest – from a perusal of public administration
materials and documents, primarily in the libraries of the Academy of
the Socialist Republic of Romania and the Law Faculty of the University
of Bucharest and secondarily in university libraries in Iaşi and Cluj-
Napoca; from contact with academics involved in the teaching and
preparation of persons for careers in public administration; and from intensive interviewing of persons involved in development administration
in the three provinces (judeţe)[5] of Cluj, Iaşi, and Buzău – that the
socialization process experienced by prospective civil servants via
university education in pre- and postwar Romania is much the same,
once one attempts to pass beyond the language of Marxist-Leninism and
to enter the realm of actual bureaucratic behavior.

Bureaucratic Controls

This is especially the case when one examines the control side of
public administration in Romania, the category called state administra-

tion (*administraţia de stat*). As a matter of fact, the most accurate translation in Romanian for what we know in the West as public administration is *administraţia de stat.* At the subnational level in every people's council (the provincial and local organs of government in which the political and administrative functions of government are fused), the *secretar* is the senior administrative official, directly under the jurisdiction of the council's executive leadership (the president, the first vice president and one or more vice presidents, depending on the size of the unit of government). Under the authority of the *secretar* is a section (*secţia*) called state administration, which functions as a staff unit in addition to its control and regulatory responsibilities. At the provincial or *judeţ* level, this unit is responsible for the control of all local people's councils within the province and operates through a series of inspectors, each assigned to a particular group of localities. At the local level there is frequently only a single *secretar* charged with responsibility for keeping local records and for seeing that the laws and directives of superior state and party organs are implemented.

At the provincial level, there are other specialized administrative units that must be taken in account. Some of them – for example, local industries and urban and rural planning (*sistematizare*) – are directly subordinated to a particular people's council, while others – those concerned with mainline administrative services in health, education, culture, and agriculture – are administered according to the principle of double subordination. Strictly speaking, no central ministry in Romania today has a field administrative service of its own. Instead, in each province there is a parallel set of offices whose employees are considered to be those of the provincial people's council and who answer to the council's executive leadership on questions of general policy and operations and to the appropriate ministry on technical questions. Usually, the *secretar* oversees the operations of these administrative units, especially in terms of their legality, while combinations of offices are placed under the authority of one of the provincial vice presidents. There are various kinds of technical personnel, according to the type of administrative unit in which they are working, but the Romanian conceptualization of the administrative function is essentially a supervisory or control one, exercised by someone trained in state administration and pursuing a career in that service. These men normally begin their careers as *secretars* in rural localities, move up through various categories of local government units, become provincial inspectors, and, if they do well, eventually end up as *secretars* at the provincial level. In the three *judeţe* where I conducted fieldwork those who were provincial *inspectors* and *secretars* either had been in these positions for many years or had moved into them with the intention of staying; the positions carried with them considerable standing within state officialdom. All those who had reached the top of this career service had at various times completed one or more advanced training courses at the Academy Ştefan Gheorghiu in Bucharest, the elite educational institution for party cadres.

Textbook Perspectives

Romanian writing on public administration reflects this concern with public law. All innovative work of a theoretical nature was being done in the law schools, where various scholars had incorporated administrative theory picked up from cross-national sources into a legal context. Examples of this newer research and writing in Romanian public administration are Alexandru Negoiţă's *Ştiinţa administraţiei* [The science of administration] and Mihai T. Oroveanu's *Introducere în ştiinţa administraţiei de stat* [Introduction to the science of state administration].[6] Both books are attuned to traditional French and German concepts of public administration, as frequently reflected in the work of those Continental specialists in public administration who identify themselves with the International Institute of Administrative Sciences in Brussels.

The one major exception to this generalization falls within the public enterprise area, but in the Romanian context administration of the nation's public enterprises constitutes an entirely different productive sector: economic activities of the state, as opposed to administrative or regulatory functions. There the prevailing literature in administration is a subcategory of economics and when international sources are turned to, they come from business administration. While there was a general unawareness of the existence of a distinct field called public administration in the United States, both in the literature researched and the interviews conducted, many party officials and academics interested in public management were widely read and up-to-date on the latest developments in U.S. business administration. The general principle followed in all this writing and in discussions of training programs was that the best international literature to use in the preparation of people for managerial roles was the West's work in business administration, modified and adapted to socialist reality (i.e., purified of its capitalist or private-sector orientation and revised according to the principles of Marxist-Leninism so that it would be of use to managers in republican industries). Thus, the standard Romanian managerial manual begins with a brief statement of the principles of Marxist-Leninism as applied to the national economy and moves very quickly into the kind of analysis common to texts in U.S. colleges of business administration.

INTERACTION BETWEEN PARTY
AND STATE BUREAUCRATS

Nowhere is the principle of democratic centralism clearer in Romania than at the subnational level: in the country's provinces (*judeţe*), cities (*oraşe*), and communes (*comune*). In describing their system to outsiders, Romanians like to stress the importance of the local government reforms of 1968, in which Soviet-style *raions* were replaced by *judeţe* (the traditional Romanian provincial units) and in which local assemblies called *sfaturi* (to emphasize Slavic ties) became known as *consilii populare* (people's councils – an expression identified more with Romania's Latin heritage).[7] Although these changes may have had an important symbolic effect in terms of Romanian nationalism, the most important structural changes were the abolition of the old prefectural system in 1949 (with its prefects, *preturi*, and *primari*, or mayors) and the creation of regional and local councils in 1950. Since that date the fusion of political and administrative functions in these councils has meant that they are, on the one hand, representative bodies made up of varying numbers of local deputies according to the territorial unit involved and, on the other, administrative institutions, headed by executive committees. Under the jurisdiction of these executive committees fall bureaucratic units responsible for implementation of the local plan and parallel organizations, duplicating the major ministries in the region and regulated according to the principle of double subordination. Furthermore, as if to remind citizens continuously of the integration of party and state, it is common practice for regional and local party organizations to be housed in the same building as the local people's council. In every instance the first secretary of the local party organization is also the president of the local people's council and the local Socialist Unity front (FUS). In most cases dual office-holding between party and state roles extends down through the ranks of the first vice president and the second vice presidents.

Uniformities and Discontinuities in
Territorial Administration

The people's councils consist of a four-tiered organizational structure: a national body charged with coordination and control responsibilities, the Council for Problems of the People's Councils (CPCP); *judeţe* organizations, with a fully developed set of administrative and political organs; city organizations; and communal organizations. Because of the extent to which the *judeţe* councils are merged with *judeţe* party organizations, the key units in this organizational structure are those operating at the provincial level, for they function as a kind of microcosm of the national government. As a rule, the council's own exclusive administrative organs are those responsible for implementation of the plan within the *judeţ* (the sections for control and state administration; planning, development, and organization; architecture and physical planning; and offices for commercial inspection, price control and fees, accounting and administration, which – as already mentioned – are administered according to the principle of double subordination).

While in theory a uniform set of administrative and political structures exists throughout the country, in practice this uniformity is confined to political organs where party and state roles are fused. Actual territorial administrative structures and practice reflect different regional priorities in planning and implementation of development policies. It is at this level that administrative practice has led to the development of several alternative policy channels that provide regional and national party leaders more flexibility in meeting program needs than is apparent on first inspection. Legal form projects the image of socialist uniformity, but administrative reality requires the implementation of a variety of different programs in a country still characterized by marked regional disparities on a par with any found in the mixed economies of developing capitalist countries.

Despite thirty years of emphasis on balanced planning and balanced development Romania remains, along with the other states of southeastern and southwestern Europe, a country characterized by great internal heterogeneity in geography, culture, and economic development. My fieldwork, extending over a two-year period, has taken me into seven very different regions of the country: pilot studies in four (Suceava in Bucovina, in northeastern Romania; Sibiu and Braşov, along the Transylvanian side of the Carpathians; and Teleorman, on the Danubian plains west of Bucharest) and in-depth fieldwork in three (Cluj, an administrative, university, and commercial center in Transylvania – an integral part of "developed" Romania; Iaşi, the former capital of Moldavia and a developing industrial center in one of the poorest regions of the country; and Buzău, east of Bucharest, in the heart of a productive agricultural area in the midst of transition as commercialized agriculture and derivative food-processing and related agricultural industries are developed.[8]

The most important industrial development projects in the country belong to what are called the republican industries; these are plants financed, built, and maintained directly by one of the central economic ministries. While regional party organizations provide connecting links in obtaining central government attention to local needs and in supervising plant operations, republican industries fall outside the administrative jurisdiction of regional people's councils. Directly under the *judeţe* people's councils are local industries and regional economic development plans—all of which belong to what is called the *plan local* as distinguished from the *plan naţional* and are financed by *judeţe* rather than republican funds. Although local industries play an important economic role in the more developed regions—for example, Cluj and Braşov—in poorer regions where economic development is a priority—such as Iaşi—the most important economic operations belong to the republican industries.

Likewise, the actual operations of organs directly subordinated to *judeţe* people's councils and those administered according to the principle of double subordination vary widely. The most notable examples encountered were the regional agricultural bureaus (Direcţii generale pentru agricultură şi industrie alimentară). In regions where there is extensive and well-developed agriculture these offices enjoy a great deal of program autonomy. In contrast, school inspectorates, health bureaus, worker and social security programs, and commercial activities—programs that also belong to the category of organs subject to double subordination—were far more likely to function as *judeţe*-based dependencies.

Bureaucratic Discretion

A final set of findings concerns variations in program operations and instances in which bureaucratic discretion, if any, was likely to be encountered at the subnational level. As might be concluded from the model provided by other socialist states in eastern Europe (except Yugoslavia), there was virtually no local autonomy encountered at the community level, except for the expression of opinions on the part of local representatives in state and party organs. All resources came from the *judeţe* level and all important decisions were made there. There were few, if any, responsibilities that could be carried out within a local community without prior approval and consent on the part of the *judeţ* people's council. In contrast to the picture presented by local government in villages, small towns, and cities—which suggests little or no room for local action and local influence, except in the most routine areas—the region (the *judeţ*) has come to provide a more open forum. The role of the *judeţ* president and the first vice president is essentially that of broker, articulating local necessities and desires, and continually seeking the allocation of new funds and supports from the central government's ministries and other institutions. The official image presented by synoptic planning and rational decision making belies the intense politicking

that goes on at the regional level between *judeţ* and community representatives and at the national level between *judeţe* officials and national
political and administrative figures.

CROSS-SYSTEM COMPARISON

Hitherto, fieldwork by social scientists in central Europe has been
either of the case-study variety or, when comparative analysis is under-
taken, of an intrasystemic nature – i.e., confined to the comparison of
one socialist state to another. Yet, if a wider economic criterion is used
(as was pointed out in the preface) one might also find it useful to draw a
different dividing line in Europe than that between East and West, a line
separating developing areas on the periphery from the more developed
central and northern regions of the continent and extending across
southern Europe from Romania to Portugal. To this perspective might
also be added some of the Latin American states, especially Mexico since
it too falls in the middle-range developing state category and is on the immediate periphery of the more developed regions of the North American
continent. Other reasons for including Mexico, for comparative purposes, are the facts that historically it has had a dependency relationship
with the United States, continues to manifest strong desires for
autonomy and a distinctive cultural identity (which make this case
somewhat analogous to the historic push-pull factors in Romanian-
Russian relations), and is also a single-party authoritarian state.

Center-Periphery Relations

While there are also obvious differences – the most notable being a
command socialist economy versus a mixed, free-market economy – let
us examine for a moment the nature of center-periphery relations in the
context of the Romanian and Mexican systems, to distinguish more
clearly between characteristics common to Romania and other eastern
European states and those that cut across southern Europe and Latin
America. Parallel field research conducted in Mexico in 1966, 1969, and
1979 confirmed the existence of a set of political and administrative relations that correspond closely to what Robert Fried identified earlier in
his study of Italian prefects as an unintegrated prefectural model.[9] This
is a style of field administration in which, while effective control authority over local affairs is vested in a prefect-governor appointed by the interior ministry, actual administrative operations provided by field services of the central ministries operate autonomously, especially in areas
within their technical competence. Using this explanatory framework
Fried singled out four characteristics: the presence of a highly centralized

government with great restrictions on local autonomy, the centering of forces resisting local autonomy with the national government's bureaucratic institutions, the presence of prefect-governors fulfilling essentially political rather than administrative roles, and the existence of substantial program autonomy within the field agencies of the central ministries operating in the same region.[10]

Expanding beyond the limits of that study, which was set in the framework of two forms of field administration systems (integrated and unintegrated prefectural systems), there are three other studies relevant to this discussion: Jerry Hough's *The Soviet Prefects* (1969), Daniel Nelson's dissertation, "Local Politics in Romania" (1975), and Sidney Tarrow's *Between Center and Periphery* (1977).[11] The Hough study suggests that the prefectural model, as developed from studies of French and Italian territorial administration by Chapman, Fesler, and Fried,[12] also has its applications in the Soviet context – as another instance of field administration in the context of highly centralized states. Hough argues that local party organs in the Soviet Union have developed analogous prefectural functions in the regulation of republican industries, although there has been a shift from individual to collective leadership.

The Significance of Field Administration

The principle of double subordination that is so frequently encountered in party-state relations in communist systems and is a crucial part of territorial administration is, as Nelson suggests, a direct corollary of democratic centralism.[13] However, leaving ideology aside and looking strictly at administrative performance, Hough suggests that in effect what operates in the various republics in the Soviet system in the area of industrial decision making is an integrated prefectural system. In it the single prefect-governor has been replaced by collective party leadership exercising overall control and regulation in the operation of republican industries, which are directly subordinated via administrative lines to central government economic ministries.

Moving beyond the historic dimensions of the Fried study, which is essentially a study of the role of the Italian prefects in the evolution of the Italian state, Tarrow gets into much more of the substance of territorial administration in France and Italy, in comparative context, than has ever been the case in previous work by calling attention to the great difference between the French *dirigiste* tradition of centralized bureaucratic control and the looser clientelistic practices of the Italian state. In fact, one review of this work has gone so far as to call the Tarrow study a seminal work in the development of a theory of field administration and center-periphery dynamics in Europe.[14]

ROMANIA IN COMPARATIVE PERSPECTIVE

What does all this suggest for Romania? If the foregoing studies of regional and local government are placed in juxtaposition with my Romanian field research, there are four conclusions that can be reached.

Integrated Field Services

First, Romanian practice in comparative perspective emerges as one of the most highly integrated instances of field administration in Europe (East and West) and the Americas. While obviously the immediately relevant state structures all fall very much within the Soviet model after 1950, Romanian field administration – if Hough's study provides an accurate point of reference – is much more attuned to the French *dirigiste* tradition, which Tarrow discusses and contrasts to the clientelistic-oriented Italian state, than to Soviet experience and actual administrative performance. Such a statement, however, must be taken as merely a first approximation, given the absence of more specific information on territorial administration in the Soviet Union. The Hough study focuses only on the relation between republican industries (industrial decision making) and regional party organizations and supplies no information about territorial administration in such areas as agricultural, health, education, and welfare services. Nelson asserts that, while an interlocking leadership between party and state organs is common to all communist systems, what is distinctive about the Romanian setting is the degree to which the local party chairman is required to be the president of the local people's council.[15]

My data, which focus on public bureaucracy and build from Nelson's data on local politics, suggest that Ceauşescu's directive regarding the merger of executive leadership roles in state and party organs (one that coincides with other alterations in Romanian state structures in the late 1960s, as the first secretary moved the country much more clearly in the direction of national communism and away from subservience to the Soviet model) revived a much older pattern of authority relations in the Romanian state. While there is an unescapable emphasis on collective decision making at all levels (and my interviews reflect that orientation on questions related to decision-making patterns in the executive committees of the *judeţe* and local people's councils), at each level it is the single executive who actually wields the most power. The parallelism in the system is striking. At the national level – as was pointed out in the preceding chapter – Ceauşescu merges in his person the position of first secretary of the party, head of state, and president of the Socialist Unity front. At the local level, the same pattern is repeated.

Reinforcing this pattern is the terminology used by my interviewees in referring to the dominant local political, administrative, and mass-organization authority: that of *primar*, literally the one who is primary or first in the community; this is the historic designation for mayor at the village level.

In terms of alternative field administration models suggested by the available literature, then, the Romanian case is one of a highly integrated prefectural system, with one modification. Romanian practice in industrial decision making, insofar as it concerns republican industries, continues to follow the Soviet model. It is here that my own data are limited and do not permit additional interpretation. This is because my approval *(adeverinţa)* for fieldwork restricted me to working within the people's councils and I could not move freely into another state sector, one in this instance that would have required approval through the economic ministries. However, in one instance questions directed at a *judeţ* first party secretary and president of the people's council (a man who was considered to be one of the most influential secretaries in the country) did suggest very close coordination of *judeţ* economic policy through his offices, continuation of the principle of double subordination into this area of industrial decision making, and hence further confirmation of the existence of a highly integrated prefectural system.

Centralized Decision Making

The second finding confirms an observation already made in using a cross-national perspective: there are few, if any, issues of importance in Romania that can be resolved at the community level. All issue resolution, except for the most routine items, either requires action at the provincial level in the administrative offices of the people's council or necessitates action in Bucharest by provincial authorities in conjunction with central government officials. As was observed in the final chapter of the Mexican state government study, so too in the Romanian context the brokerage functions of the region's political leaders are crucial. Whereas the emphasis given to plan design and execution each year is extremely important in fixing development priorities throughout the country, it is no less true in the Romanian case than in the Mexican that "successful issue resolution requires the maintenance of linkages and communication networks on a vertical and horizontal basis — vertically between the community and the [provincial] government and the nation's capital; horizontally, between the mayor and the major interests in the community; and among the [*judeţ* president], the major groups in the [province], and [national] authorities who have the resources to resolve the issues at hand."[16] The mainspring of the system at each level–community and province–was the executive committee and within it the individual who was both first secretary and people's council president.

Centralized Finances

Third, financial resources are concentrated at the center and distributed between center and periphery through the *județe* people's councils. The critical battles for financial resources are those between one *județ* organization and another, vis-à-vis national state and party organs. Individual communities have few, if any, resources of their own and are totally dependent on accommodations worked out in the *județ* capital. A few figures will illustrate this point. In the 1978 national budget (*buget de stat*), 84 percent of public funds were assigned to the republican budget (268,922.9 million *lei*) with the remainder going to the local budgets–those of the *județe* and, within these, to municipalities and communes (49,578.4 million *lei*). Since great discrepancies exist among the *județe* in terms of their development, an important part of the distribution of national resources in the provinces comes in the form of subventions from the republican budget for *bugetele locale* of the lesser developed *județe*.

An example of how these resources are distributed can be seen in the 1978 budget for the *județe* in which I did my fieldwork. In that document, the *județe* are ranked in terms of the size of their local budgets, from the lowest to the highest. In this ranking, Buzău was in tenth place; Cluj in twelfth; and Iași in twenty-second, out of a total of thirty-nine *județe* plus the municipality of Bucharest. The actual breakdown in thousands of *lei* was: Buzău with 1,208,167 (of which 473,872 was funded out of local receipts); Cluj with 1,157,610 (of which 969,611 was funded out of local receipts), and Iași with 2,006,395 (of which 618,666 was funded out of local receipts). In fortieth place was Bucharest with 4,707,012 (of which 3,305,473 was funded out of local receipts).[17]

The discrepancy between the amount funded out of local receipts and the total amount allotted, however, should not be confused with direct subventions. The portion left over here entails regularly designated republican funding. In fiscal year 1978, sixteen of the thirty-nine *județe* did receive direct subventions (*subvențiile*). Of the three in which I worked, only one–Buzău–was provided with a subvention (148,000 *lei*). As for budgets internal to the *județe*, I was able to collect data in only one instance–Cluj–for the same year. In that case there were sixty-nine communes, three cities, and three municipalities. These internal *județ* figures show the same variation in public finance, with every community receiving varying amounts for its local operating budget from above (*subvenţii din buget ierarhic superior*). Accordingly, if one adds the instances of direct subventions to those in which republic funding is already designated in the normal year-to-year budget, the reliance on the central government for financial resources is overwhelming. Only the more developed *judeţe* can supplement republican funds with local funds.

Regional Disparities

Fourth, after thirty years of balanced planning and a policy of leveling regional differences, Romania remains a country with highly skewed internal differentiation. This is not to deny marked economic progress over this period, for there has been real and substantial economic growth as Romania has moved from the status of an underdeveloped agrarian state in the direction of a commercialized agriculture and an industrial economy. Development—*dezvoltare*—has been and continues to be a stated goal, constantly receiving emphasis. But the point is, when Romania is compared with other middle-range developing countries, its successes under socialism have not been all that different from those instances in which unbalanced growth strategies under mixed economies have been pursued. The data contained in the following three tables capture these patterns quite well. Table 4.1 reflects changes in employment patterns for Romania as a whole over a twenty-six-year period (1950–1976); Table 4.2 provides a breakdown of industrial production by *judeţe*, which clearly shows the primacy of Bucharest over any other single area in the country; and Table 4.3 gives the distribution of the work force by *judeţe*. The only city that comes close to the level of industrialization achieved by Bucharest is Braşov. As a matter of fact, Ion Blaga, one of the two basic sources in Romanian on variation in internal socioeconomic development, concludes after looking at various statistical indices that Bucharest and Braşov alone in Romania can be placed in a category with the more developed socialist countries.[18] While there are other important urban centers in Romania, none approaches the industrial importance of these two centers except Prahova, the *judeţ* where Ploieşti is situated, which is the seat of Romania's petrochemical industry.

CONCLUSIONS

While much more could be done with the data collected from fieldwork at the subnational level, there is no reason here to pursue it further. It would neither alter the conclusions reached above nor assist the reader in obtaining a more comprehensive understanding of the

TABLE 4.1

EMPLOYMENT BY BRANCH OF NATIONAL INDUSTRY (%)

		1950	1955	1960	1965	1970	1975	1976
1.	Industry	12.0	13.1	15.1	19.2	25.0	30.6	31.9
2.	Construction	2.2	4.3	4.9	6.3	7.8	8.1	8.3
3.	Agriculture	74.1	69.5	65.4	56.5	49.1	37.8	35.6
4.	Forestry	0.2	0.2	0.2	0.2	0.2	0.3	0.3
5.	Transportation	1.9	2.4	2.4	3.1	3.7	4.3	4.3
6.	Telecommunications	0.3	0.3	0.4	0.6	0.6	0.7	0.7
7.	Merchandising	2.5	3.3	3.4	4.0	4.3	5.5	5.8
8.	Urban services	0.7	0.9	1.5	2.1	3.0	3.4	3.5
9.	Teaching & cultural affairs	2.3	2.2	2.7	3.5	3.7	4.0	4.1
10.	Science & scientific services	0.2	0.3	0.4	0.5	0.5	0.8	0.8
11.	Health care, social assistance & physical education	1.1	1.2	1.6	2.0	2.3	2.6	2.7
12.	Administration	1.7	1.5	1.2	1.0	0.7	0.7	0.7
13.	Other activities	0.8	0.8	0.8	1.0	1.1	1.2	1.3

Source: Anuarul statistic al Republicii Socialiste România [Statistical yearbook of the Socialist Republic of Romania] , 1977, p. 101.

dynamics of government and politics in Romania at the subnational level. To move further into the interview material would necessitate entry into specialized single-country or case-study material and neglect the larger setting.

The essential point to be established here is that despite the great social, political, and economic change entailed in moving from a mixed free-market economy to a command-socialist economy, and despite the tremendous human costs (liquidating previously dominant social classes and recruiting new government personnel meeting the tripartite

TABLE 4.2

PERCENTAGE OF AGGREGATE NATIONAL PRODUCTION BY JUDEȚE

	Județ	1965	1970	1975
1.	Albă	1.6	1.4	1.4
2.	Arad	2.8	2.2	2.0
3.	Arges	2.2	3.2	3.7
4.	Bacău	3.9	3.4	2.8
5.	Bihor	2.3	2.4	2.4
6.	Bistrița-Năsăud	0.4	0.3	0.3
7.	Botoșani	0.6	0.6	0.6
8.	Brașov	6.3	6.7	6.5
9.	Brăila	2.1	2.1	1.9
10.	Buzău	0.9	1.1	1.5
11.	Caraș-Severin	3.3	2.7	2.0
12.	Cluj	3.3	3.5	3.5
13.	Constanța	1.9	2.1	2.2
14.	Covasna	0.6	0.5	0.6
15.	Dimbrovița	1.7	1.5	1.9
16.	Dolj	2.3	3.2	3.1
17.	Galați	1.9	3.2	4.3
18.	Gorj	0.8	1.1	1.0
19.	Harghița	1.2	1.0	1.1
20.	Hunedoara	6.2	5.2	3.7
21.	Ialomița	0.6	0.9	0.9
22.	Iași	2.2	2.8	3.3
23.	Ilfov	1.4	1.3	1.3
24.	Maramureș	2.3	1.9	1.3
25.	Mehedinți	0.8	0.8	1.1
26.	Mureș	3.4	3.4	2.0
27.	Neamț	2.6	2.6	2.7
28.	Olt	0.9	1.1	2.3
29.	Prahova	7.0	6.3	5.5
30.	Satu Mare	1.2	1.1	2.3
31.	Sălaj	0.3	1.2	0.3
32.	Sibiu	3.6	3.6	3.6
33.	Suceava	2.0	1.8	1.7
34.	Teleorman	0.9	0.9	1.2
35.	Timiș	3.8	3.6	3.5
36.	Tulcea	0.5	0.5	0.5
37.	Vaslui	0.7	0.7	0.8
38.	Vîlcea	0.8	0.9	1.0
39.	Vrancea	0.9	0.7	0.7
40.	Municipiul București	17.8	17.5	17.6

Source: Vasile Rausser (coord.), Repartizarea teritoriala ă industriei [The territorial distribution of industry] (București: Editura Academiei Republicii Soicaliste România, 1977), p. 44.

TABLE 4.3

RANKINGS OF <u>JUDEŢE</u> ON THE BASIS OF WORKERS PER 1000 INHABITANTS (1972)

1. 0 to 150 . . . . Botoşani, Sălaj, Vaslui, Teleorman.

2. 151 to 210 . . . Suceava, Bistriţa-Năsăud, Neamţ, Vrancea, Buzău,
                     Olt, Mehedinţi, Ilfov.

3. 211 to 280 . . . Satu Mare, Maramureş, Bihor, Mureş, Harghiţa, Bacău,
                     Covasna, Gorj, Vîlcea, Dolj, Ialomiţa, Tulcea,
                     Dîmbroviţa, Albă, Iaşi.

4. 281 to 350 . . . Cluj, Arad, Hunedoara, Caraş-Severin, Argeş, Prahova,
                     Galaţi, Brăila.

5. Over 350 . . . Sibiu, Timiş, Braşov, Constanţa, Bucureşti.

Source: Ion Blaga, <u>Repartizarea teritoriala ă fortelor de producţie în
          România: Problema şi soluţiile ei</u> [The territorial distribution
          of the forces of production in Romania: the problem and its
          solutions] (Bucureşti: Editura ştiinţifică, 1974), p. 45.

qualifications of party membership, personal allegiance to the ruler, and technical qualifications), Romania is not notably better off than other countries whose aggregate indices approximate its own. The crucial changes involve movement from one form of dependency to another and recognition that, whether under socialism or capitalism, this century's latecomers to the Industrial Revolution are finding it increasingly difficult to carve out a viable national space within which to consolidate that modicum of economic self-sufficiency essential to real state autonomy. None of this is intended to minimize Romanian accomplishments over the previous thirty years, for when one examines aggregate indices of productivity the changes have been great. In the past Romania was an underdeveloped agrarian society with a limited number of industrial enclaves. Today it is a middle-range developing country with important industrial and commercial activities of its own making, achieved in large part despite COMECON preferences that it maximize its agricultural and natural-resource potential and rely on others in the Eastern bloc for its more sophisticated industrial needs. In building national communism in Romania that option has always been unacceptable. Despite differences in personal leadership style, as one moves from the 1950s through the 1970s, the commitment of the party's top leadership to national development has remained unaltered. Accepting as a given the present pattern of dependency and the need to maintain ideological orthodoxy, this leadership (despite the entrance and exit of diverse personalities) has focused its objectives on economic development as the solution to Romania's historic problems of underdevelopment and subservience to those powers dominant in the regime. The problem is that as the regime is entering the 1980s it is finding that it is rapidly exhausting its potential for further growth under the present model.

While the barriers to comparative analysis are formidable once one attempts to span the dividing line between Eastern and Western Europe, I suspect we cannot advance further in our understanding of the dynamics of the Balkan states until we abandon the constraints under which we have been operating since World War II. The essence of comparative analysis entails isolating similarities and differences. Yet, so long as the analysis of countries such as Romania is confined to one category of state–in this instance East European communist regimes–few advances can be made. In short, given the evolution of scholarship on the developing world since World War II, the time has come to begin more systematic comparative analysis of national experiences under mixed-economy, free-market countries and those of the socialist world and, within them, the investigation of alternative administrative structures and practices utilized to meet more effectively development objectives.

NOTES

1. Lajos Szamel, *Legal Problems of Socialist Public Administrative Management* (transl. by G. Pulay) (Budapest: Akadémiai Kiadó, 1973), p. 69.

2. In addition to the Szamel source cited above, see Andrew C. Janos, "Modernization and Decay in Historical Perspective: The Case of Romania" in Kenneth Jowitt, ed., *Social Change in Romania, 1860–1940: A Debate on Development in a European Nation* (Berkeley: Institute of International Studies, University of California, 1978), pp. 72–116; and Stefan M. Zeletin, *Burghezia română: Origina și rolul ei istoric* [The Romanian bourgeoisie: their origin and historic role] (București: Bibliotecă socială, 1925).

3. Milovan Djilas, *The New Class: An Analysis of the Communist System* (New York: Praeger Publishers, 1957).

4. The most recent statement of the formal organizational structure of Romanian public bureaucracy is contained in Decree 396/1976 and supplemental Council of State legislation (Decree Nos. 397, 398, 399, 400 of December 7, 1976). Missing from this list of the major organizational units are those ministries in

which no changes were made in 1976: the ministries of interior, defense, and foreign affairs. The addition of these entities brings the total to thirty-nine.

5. For more accurate cross-national comparative purposes, I am using the term "province" as the English-language equivalent of *judeţ*, even though official Romanian publications prefer to translate the word as "county," to avoid confusion with earlier historic governmental units of the same name.

6. Alexandru Negoiţa, *Ştiinţa administraţiei* [The science of administration] (Bucureşti: Editura didactică şi pedagogică, 1977) and Mihai T. Oroveanu, *Introducere în ştiinţa administraţiei de stat* [Introduction to the science of state administration] (Bucureşti: Editura enciclopedică română, 1975).

7. In these changes the four-tiered Soviet-style system of regions, *raions,* cities, and communes was replaced with a three-tiered one of *judeţe,* cities, and communes. Technically there is a difference in category between municipality and *oraş* (town), but this refers to city size and status only.

8. This field work was done in several phases: first during a preliminary field trip around Romania in January 1977 (to Suceava, Cluj, Sibiu, Braşov, and Buzău); a short visit to Teleorman in December 1977; and in-depth fieldwork in Cluj, Iaşi, and Buzău, April–July 1978.

9. See Lawrence S. Graham, *Politics in a Mexican Community* (Gainesville: University of Florida Press, 1968) and *Mexican State Government: A Prefectural System in Action* (Austin: Institute of Public Affairs, University of Texas, 1971). The 1968 study took place in Celya, Guanajuato; the 1971 study, in Morelia, Michoacán, and surrounding communities. In the summer of 1979 I returned to Mexico for additional fieldwork in Oaxaca, Oaxaca, and Villahermosa, Tabasco. As in the case of the Michoacán study, side trips were made to surrounding communities.

10. Graham, *Mexican State Government,* p. 67.

11. Jerry F. Hough, *The Soviet Prefects: The Local Party Organs in Industrial Decision-Making* (Cambridge: Harvard University Press, 1969); Daniel Newlyn Nelson, "Local Politics in Romania: An Intra-National Comparison" (unpublished doctoral dissertation: Johns Hopkins University, 1975); Sidney Tarrow, *Between Center and Periphery: Grassroots Politicians in Italy and France* (New Haven: Yale University Press, 1977).

12. James W. Fesler, "The Political Role of Field Administration," in *Papers in Comparative Public Administration,* edited by Ferrell Heady and Sybil L. Stokes (Ann Arbor: Institute of Public Administration, University of Michigan, 1962), pp. 117–143; Robert C. Fried, *The Italian Prefects: A Study in Administrative Politics* (New Haven: Yale University Press, 1963); and Brian Chapman, *The Prefects and Provincial France* (London: Allen and Unwin, 1955).

13. Nelson, "Local Politics," p. 80.

14. Sidney Tarrow, *Between Center and Periphery: Grassroots Politicians in Italy and France,* as reviewed by Robert D. Putnam in *American Political Science Review* 72:3 (September 1978), pp. 1134–1135.

15. Nelson, "Local Politics," p. 74.

16. Graham, *Mexican State Government,* pp. 67–68. Brackets have been imposed where specific Mexican terminology should be replaced by a Romanian

term to call attention to parallelism in state structures in such cases once one moves beyond the level of specific country terminology.

17. *Buletinul oficial* [The official bulletin] (Anul XIII, Nr. 129, Partea I, vineri 2/XII/1977), pp. 11–12.

18. Ion Blaga, *Repartizarea teritorială a forțelor de producție în România: problema și soluțiile ei* [The territorial distribution of the forces of production in Romania: the problem and its solutions] (București: Editura științifica, 1974), p. 88.

5

External Relations: Leninist Dependency and the Outside World

Intertwined with the emphasis on socioeconomic development and the goal of autarky has been the cultivation of an independent foreign policy. Since the 1960s this has entailed three fundamental aspects: the projection of national interests above those identified with international communism and the Soviet Union as the primary interpreter of socialist bloc policy; good relations with countervailing centers of world power, to offset Soviet influence over internal affairs; and a multilateral foreign policy, defined as cordial relations with as wide a range of states as possible and special concern with developing nations.

REDUCING SOVIET INFLUENCE OVER INTERNAL AFFAIRS

From the time of the Sino-Soviet split, Romanian foreign policy has emphasized consistently national autonomy within the socialist bloc. In economic affairs this has meant resistance to Soviet pressures for closer integration of the Romanian economy with COMECON; in military affairs it has meant refusal to participate in Warsaw Pact operations elsewhere in eastern Europe and most notably to permit joint pact troop maneuvers on Romanian territory. When Russia intervened in Czechoslovakia in 1968 Ceauşescu issued strong criticism of Soviet actions and reaffirmed Romania's determination to resist a similar incursion into its own national territory. More than a decade later this stance remained equally strong, as evidenced by Ceauşescu's decision to air publicly his divergences with Brezhnev and the Soviet Union immediately after the November 1979 meeting of the Warsaw Pact countries in Moscow. These entailed Romanian differences with the Soviet Union over its Middle Eastern policy and its desire to have it ratified by the East European states, resistance to Soviet pressure for increased military expenditures in Eastern Europe, and opposition to Soviet wishes for more effective integration of the region's military forces under Soviet leadership in the event of an emergency. Other manifestations of this stance vis-à-vis the Soviet Union have been continued Romanian opposition to the idea of Soviet use of Romanian territory to deploy troops in Bulgaria or elsewhere in the Balkans in the event of conflict; refusal for over a decade to sever relations with Israel, despite Soviet policy of condemning Israeli actions and seeking an accommodation with the Arab states; close relations with Yugoslavia; consistent attacks on the existence of military blocs and the maintenance of foreign bases and foreign troops in other countries; and criticism of the Soviet invasion of Afghanistan in 1980.

Multilateral Foreign Relations

To effect this combined policy of autarky and an independent foreign policy, close relations with countervailing centers of world power have become essential to offset Soviet influence. The most important of these has been the relationship with China. Throughout the Sino-Soviet controversy Romania has consistently taken a pro-Chinese position – in ideological questions, in questions of foreign policy, in cultural and economic affairs. In ideological terms, this has meant identification with the right of national communist parties to reinterpret Marxist-Leninist principles in accordance with national conditions; in foreign policy questions, it has meant support for Chinese criticism of aggressive Soviet stances and siding with the Chinese on questions of Vietnamese policy both before and after the U.S. withdrawal from Indochina; the regular exchange of high-level diplomatic missions and visits; the promotion of cultural exchanges; and economic cooperation and trade where feasible and mutually beneficial.

Second only to close relations with China has been the cultivation of good relations with the West, notably the United States, the Federal Republic of Germany, the United Kingdom, and France. While these relations are more restricted because of the ideological problem presented by contact with capitalist countries and the desire to control the amount of Western influence over nationals, the promotion of diplomatic, economic, and cultural ties with these countries is very important to the Romanian regime. The easiest aspect of this policy to implement has been good diplomatic relations and the promotion of high-level state visits, such as the various visits of Western heads of state to Romania and Ceauşescu's visits abroad. Closely linked to this continual flurry of diplomatic activity has been the promotion of increased trade with the West, loans and credits, and the import of technology and know-how. Today trading relations run the gamut from agricultural produce marketed in Western Europe to clothing, footwear, and furniture, to more specialized industrial production (viz, the contract with France and the United Kingdom to produce helicopters). The development of a national automotive industry has come about in large part through cooperation with Renault of France, in the purchase of equipment and the contracting of French technicians to produce the Romanian Dacia. Likewise, there are a number of specific U.S. operations, ranging from the authorization given to Manufacturers Hanover Trust Company to operate a Bucharest branch for the purpose of financing and handling credits necessary to facilitate Romanian trade with the West to joint ventures.

Trade Diversification

To facilitate trade with the West, and with the United States in particular, the Romanian government has taken a number of specific actions that warrant mentioning. Beginning in the mid-1960s, legislation was passed to set up a more efficient foreign trade system. Out of this legislation came the formation of a national tourist office (ONT) in 1967, the creation of the Romanian Bank of Foreign Trade in 1968, and the introduction of industrial centrals in 1969. The latter reform involved the grouping together of enterprises with similar structures, functions, or products for the purpose of promoting joint operations. In 1971 Romania joined the General Agreement on Tariffs and Trade (GATT) after fourteen years with observer status. In 1972 it became a member of the World Bank (the International Bank for Reconstruction and Development, IBRD) and the International Monetary Fund (IMF). That same year it reorganized and expanded its chambers of commerce and industry and Ministry of Foreign Trade (renamed the Ministry of Foreign Trade and International Economic Cooperation). Along with these actions went a 1971 authorization permitting Western companies to open commercial offices in Romania or to be represented by counterpart Romanian organizations, as well as a new comprehensive foreign trade law that same year. On the U.S. side, facilitating trade with Romania was the Export Administration Act of 1969, which declared it U.S. policy to encourage trade with all nations with whom the United States has diplomatic relations, and President Nixon's visit to Romania in 1969. In 1971 Nixon permitted the Export-Import Bank to extend partial credits to help finance U.S. exports to Romania. This was followed the next year by his authorization of the Overseas Private Investment Corporation to provide insurance and assistance to U.S. companies wishing to enter into investment projects in Romania. All this culminated in 1974 with the formation of the Romanian-United States Economic Council, under the joint sponsorship of Romanian and U.S. chambers of commerce, for the purpose of promoting commercial exchanges between the two countries.

Out of this context has come the formation of several cooperative agreements. The most important of these is the April 1973 joint venture contract between Control Data Corporation and the Industrial Central of Electronics and Automatization, a Romanian state enterprise.[1] Despite the hope that this agreement would soon be followed by others, it remains the only instance to date of an actual joint venture program in operation. The others fall in the category of technical assistance agreements—contracts with General Tire and Rollway Bearing International, Inc. In addition, there are a number of representatives of multinationals in Bucharest where specific trade agreements are in effect and a management consultant office maintained by Moody International Corporation, a firm with longstanding commercial contacts in Romania that represents a number of other U.S. companies doing business in Romania.

Paralleling U.S.–Romanian trading relations are numerous other contacts with West German, French, English, and Japanese nationals—all a part of the policy of diversification of economic relations with the major industrial nations.

Scientific Relations

In a similar fashion, scientific and cultural accords with the major Western countries have been promoted—notably with the United States, the United Kingdom, France, and West Germany. Again, using the U.S. example, they complement the policy of promoting cordial relations with the Western countries as well as gaining access to new scientific and technical know-how. Leaving aside strictly cultural programs in the arts and letters, which operate under the auspices of the Fulbright program in conjunction with the Ministry of Education (since there is no binational commission in Romania), the overall agency coordinating exchanges and research in the natural and social sciences is the National Council for Science and Technology (NCST). Established in 1966, the NCST's programs got underway in conjunction with the other changes that contributed to the optimism of the late 1960s and were related to the building of national communism. By the end of the NCST's first five-year plan (1966–1970), a general program and set of policies was in place for regulating all scientific and technological research, in accord with the general 1966–1970 five-year plan for the country's economic and social development.

Just as 1969 signalled important changes in Romanian policy vis-à-vis economic relations with the West, so too that year marked an important shift in programs linked to scientific and technological activities. As is so often the case with an important shift in policy, the primary point of reference is a party conference and a major address by the first secretary—in this instance the Tenth Party Congress (1969) and Ceauşescu's report to that meeting. Again, as is always the case with such shifts in policy, his words and the particular phrasing given to the directive become a crucial reference point for tracing all later developments. In this instance Ceauşescu set the tune in the following way:

> Research work should contribute directly to the increase of raw materials and resources for energy production, to conceiving new technologies, new varieties of plants and breeds of animals, new consumer goods, and to the requirements of society according to the program for the country's economic and social development.[2]

This party congress and Ceauşescu's statement regarding the place of scientific research in a developing socialist society have provided the basic frame of reference for scientific research ever since. In turn, they establish the framework through which academic exchange programs continue to operate.

Until 1969, the preeminent research institution was the Academy of the Socialist Republic of Romania. Although established originally in the mode of the French Academy and the intellectual institution par excellence for Romanian scholars trained in the French academic tradition, with the transition to socialism after the war and the heavy reliance on Soviet institutional models during the 1950s, the Romanian Academy was reshaped in accordance with the model provided by the Soviet Academy of Sciences. Like the Soviet Academy, it was headed by a Presidium under whose auspices were a wide range of semiautonomous research institutes spanning the natural and social sciences. As in the Soviet case, while the actual work produced by historians continued the tradition of a narrative style of writing more attuned to the humanities in the West than to the newer emphasis on quantitative materials and approaches identified with the social sciences, this field was recognized as an important part of the social sciences. As with the Soviet Academy, the rank of academician became the most esteemed academic honor in the country, except for the limited number of specific titles given by the state to outstanding individuals. Along with this privileged status went a substantial amount of autonomy, especially in those scientific fields recognized as of priority for the nation's development and falling in the category of the "pure" sciences as opposed to the "human" sciences.

Under Ceauşescu, however, the Romanian Academy has entered a long period of decline as the substance of responsibility for scientific research, funding, and programs has been shifted to the National Council for Science and Technology (NCST). Today, as a consequence, the Romanian Academy remains a largely honorific institution, although it still is the seat of the country's most important research library and operates a major scholarly press. But even its honorific status has been eroded as other academies have been created with the same structure of corresponding and full members, with virtually no ties to the Romanian Academy. Such is the case of the Academy of Social and Political Sciences. At the outset, the NCST focused primarily on the natural sciences in conjunction with the priority given to moving all the major research institutes in the natural sciences, agriculture, and engineering out from under the jurisdiction of the Romanian Academy. By the 1970s the social sciences were recognized as an equally important aspect of the nation's scientific research program, particularly as social engineering perspectives came into vogue. Thus, in the 1971–1980 Program for Scientific Research and Technological Development specific provision was made for the social sciences. Again, direct quotes from the plan sum up the perspective adopted and the current policy:

> Sociological research will focus on changes in Romanian social structure as reflected in rural environments and the process of urbanization. It will also deal with the improvement of investigative methodologies.
>
> Social science and humanities research also covers complex and varied activities in history, philosophy, psychology, logic, law, archeology and history of the arts. Such research is included in a program worked out and coordinated by the Academy of Social and Political Sciences.[3]

Whereas prior to the 1970s the Romanian Academy enjoyed a great deal of say-so over scientific research priorities and freedom of action in scientific and technical fields where questions of social policy were not at stake, the NCST model has been characterized by the determination of the Ceauşescu regime to control intellectual life as rigorously as it does all other aspects of society. Even though the label "Stalinist" has been used uniformly to characterize rule by the PCR as institutionalization of this particular regime of national communism has taken place, under Gheorghiu-Dej there was apparently much more tolerance and understanding of the need to keep questions of ideology and social policy out of pure research. But today there can be no question as to the extent to which party control permeates and regulates all aspects of intellectual life. To quote again from the NCST report, "Romanian research and development is conducted on the basis of directives of the Romanian Communist Party under direct leadership of Party and State bodies, and in accordance with Law Number 28/1969 'Concerning the Organization of Scientific Research.'"[4] While the principle of party leadership in all areas of life has its justification in terms of Stalinist values, in many areas—in the sciences as well as the arts—it has had a devastating effect on the quality of research and performance. As a consequence, rumors and stories abound of the priority given to party loyalty and party activists over the maintenance of rigorous professional standards.

Research and Development Policy

In determining scientific research priorities, the same values predominate as those developed for the wider society and current institutional relationships insure a close working relationship between state and party organs. Following the model discussed in Chapter 3, whereby joint party and state organs regulate and control various areas of national life, the same principle operates here. In this case, identical legalistic perspectives are used in determining specific applications and providing program directives. Accordingly, the National Council for Science and Technology has been designated as the party and state organ, subordinated directly to the Central Committee of the party, with exclusive responsibility for fulfilling party and state policy in science and technology.[5] While official language stresses cooperation with other major institutions, the NCST in effect dictates policy for the Academy of the Socialist Republic of Romania, the various academies of science (now independent of the Romanian Academy), and the research institutes (which also have become independent of the Romanian Academy). In accord with the general state model used in Romania, the research institutes are also subjected to the principle of dual subordination. Each answers to the academy designated by the state as responsible for determining research priorities and funding in its field and to the appropriate university institution whose teaching responsibilities are related to its research activities. Since many of the senior research personnel are also university teachers, dual subordination means also dual office-holding.

Following the principle of collective leadership, the policymaking body for the NCST consists of a president, a first vice president, several vice presidents appointed within the NCST, the president of the

Academy of the Socialist Republic of Romania, the presidents of the academies of sciences, the president of the State Committee for Nuclear Energy, and directors-general of the central research institutes. Its members are proposed by the NCST president and appointed by the Council of Ministers for four-year terms. Again, in practice, as is the case with all other major party and state administrative roles, policymaking responsibility is actually vested in a single person, the NCST president. Further insuring the subordination of all other research institutions to the NCST has been the practice of not replacing the president of the Romanian Academy or its senior officials after their deaths or retirement. As a consequence, even in the restricted area of cultural and scientific exchanges, where the Romanian Academy has international agreements predating these changes, the necessity of clearance and approval from above has had the effect of so embedding nationals with red tape and delays that the principle of cultural and scientific exchange has become virtually a one-way proposition, with few Romanians approved for visits abroad. From the U.S. side, its nominees are subjected to constraints not present in the more recent International Research and Exchanges Board (IREX) accord, which exists directly with the NCST.

Just as a clearcut hierarchy of authority operates in determining relations between national and subnational units of government (as outlined in the preceding chapter) so too a hierarchy of authority determines academic research operations. If CPCP is the key state-party organ for the people's councils, the NCST is the state-party institution for all programs related to the sciences and technology. Subordinated to its jurisdiction are the Romanian Institute of Standardization; the State Office for Inventions, Patents, and Trade Marks; the National Institute for Information and Documentation; eleven central research institutes; and four academies of sciences (the Romanian Academy, now subordinated to the Education Ministry; the Academy of Social and Political Sciences, whose status as an organ directly subordinated to the Central Committee of the PCR gives it a strategic advantage over the Romanian Academy; the Academy for Agricultural and Forestry Sciences, subordinated to the Ministry of Agriculture and Food Industries; and the Academy of Medical Sciences, subordinated to the Health Ministry). Aside from the policy intent of providing coordination in science and technology, the NCST and its subordinate organs have an important control function. Despite its extensive commitment to the exchange of scientific and technical personnel and its expansion to include cultural affairs, these programs operate essentially as devices for bringing outsiders to Romania, not as vehicles for permitting Romanians to make scientific trips abroad. Behind the few academics approved for such visits stand hundreds of others who would initiate contact or whose visits never come to fruition for one reason or another, ranging from failure to clear preliminary hurdles to last-minute delays arising from other organs responsible for exit visas or individual surveillance. Good relations with the Western countries may well be an ostensible goal, but against this intent one must always set the state's fear of the defection of those it approves for visits outside the socialist bloc and its suspicion that open contact with the West may subvert the commitment of its own nationals to socialist construction.

Educational Practices: Internal versus External Realities

As one moves down through the educational hierarchy – from academy to university, *lycée* to primary school – and away from external contacts, awareness of stringent controls over academic life for nationals increases. From early on students are thoroughly and continuously subjected to Marxist-Leninist ideology. Every dimension of education has its official interpretation and carefully prescribed curriculum. Ideological sessions and continuous study of Central Committee dictates pervade the entire educational establishment, with hours set aside in all offices and programs for indoctrination and discussion of the latest party policies. The form prescribed for education continues in a European mold with early career selection being an honored value – such as the selection of a secondary school with scientific curriculum for students destined to pursue a career in the sciences or a music school for those deciding on a career in the performing arts. Whatever the direction a student decides on, once he or she enters a secondary school tremendous pressure is exerted to perform at one's best. For the bright, the talented, the skilled in mathematics or sports, the rewards are great. But students who drop by the wayside or are left behind exist in numbers that those attuned to more humanistic educational values would find unacceptable.

Crossing the threshold into higher education is even more restricted. For every vacant place in a beginning university class there are numerous applicants. Again, however, it is important to understand that this elitist structure to higher education follows not more recent dictates of party policy but earlier, prewar institutional modeling after Continental European educational norms. The difference is that, as in other aspects of society, the entire educational system has been redirected to fit the needs of socialist construction. If, as in France, important decisions are made at the outset in deciding by examination whether or not to admit a student into a university course of study, the Romanian state has gone one step further by committing itself to providing employment for every university graduate. Ideally those at the top of graduating classes have the pick of the best jobs available in a given field, with those at the bottom most likely receiving undesirable work assignments in the provinces. In practice, however, stories circulate of favors being granted at all levels to the sons and daughters of party officials. For the nonelite, even if one has assiduously followed the performance norms required and faithfully participated in party organizations for the young, graduation at the top of one's class may well produce the anomaly of an unexpected assignment to an isolated rural area and the allocation of a desired position to someone else with a lower ranking in the class but enjoying the recommendation of a relative or close family friend with party connections. In short, educational forms emphasize excellence in all aspects of student life, while the reality is far too often a Byzantine maze of subtle signs and nuances that give favored status to the children of the new establishment.

It should surprise no one that this combination of indoctrination, discipline, pressure to perform, and privilege has over time begun to produce cultural malaise. While the values of extreme centralization and close control over citizens' lives have their place and justification in terms of the goals of building a new society radically different from the old, one may question the ability of this society to raise performance levels further as new generations come to the fore farther and farther removed from the traumatic experiences of the late 1930s, the 1940s, and the early 1950s. While it is difficult, if not impossible, to sample this aspect of Romanian society in quantitative terms, day-to-day contact with nationals readily introduces one to a world where cynicism, external conformity, resistance (often quiet but at times suddenly and unexpectedly manifest) abound. All this affects academic exchange programs, for research and development policies, internal educational practices, and related external contacts constitute inseparable parts of a common educational policy core.

Third World Relations

Leaving aside further discussion of internal academic life and returning to the realm of contacts with the outside world – an equally important aspect of Romania's commitment to an independent foreign policy is good relations with Third World countries. This takes the form of extensive opportunities given to Third World students, especially those from the African nations, to study in Romania. Consequently, in all the country's major universities one encounters many African students. Likewise, Romania engages in technical assistance; again, administered primarily to the African states, with priority given to those regimes where a commitment to socialism has already been made – viz, the supports provided in finance, equipment, and technical personnel for Angola and Mozambique. While most of the foreign students coming to Romania are placed in professional programs, there are also specialized courses offered for party members from the African states in the party's school for cadre training, the Academy Ştefan Gheorghiu. Finally, a significant aspect of this cult of good relations with the outside world has been Ceauşescu's policy of providing mediatory services, when possible, between Egypt and Israel and frequent regime reference to this service as an example of Romanian commitment to good relations on as broad a base as possible and to world peace.

Overall Assessment

When one checks the substance of Romanian action in areas such as these against declared intent, one must not conclude too quickly that Romania constitutes a deviant case, an instance where national autonomy of the sort impossible in Czechoslovakia has become possible. Good relations within the socialist bloc remain a major priority and, while Romania may challenge the Soviet Union on specific points that intrude directly and visibly on national sovereignty, informally there never has been a doubt on Russia's part of the commitment of the Romanian leadership to orthodox principles of Marxist-Leninism as defined by the Soviet Union. If in November 1978 Romania gave great publicity to its opposition to Soviet pressures related to its Warsaw Pact and COMECON policies, economically as well as ideologically, a close dependency relationship continues. Although Romania has diversified its trade, the Soviet Union remains its most important market and supply source. To this must be added the fact that as Romania's own petroleum reserves have declined and as the date approaches when national petroleum production will cease to be of consequence in the national economy, reliance on the Soviet Union for energy sources has increased. This was observable for the first time during early 1979 when there was shortage of heating oil (as in the previous year), shortages of gas for motor vehicles, and—by summer—the imposition of the requirement that tourists from socialist bloc countries passing through the country must, as Western tourists do, pay for their purchase in hard (i.e., Western) currency.

LIMITS TO NATIONAL AUTONOMY UNDER LENINIST DEPENDENCY[6]

In examining Romania's external relations—its declarations as well as its actions—one is able to gain additional insight into the nature of the regime. But, more so in Romania than in other states, its foreign policy must be interpreted in light of its internal policies; otherwise one may well miss some of the most important dimensions of this regime.

Nicolae Ceaușescu, as his predecessor, remains an orthodox Marxist-Leninist with a thorough commitment to the consolidation of a regime of national communism. The present leadership desires not so much to break with the socialist bloc as it does to consolidate within it a margin of autonomy, so that while cooperating with the Soviet Union on fundamentals it can become a thoroughly national regime, identified with the majority of the population. One may speculate what it would be like if the option existed of a free choice to determine its own policies, but that luxury has never existed and shows no sign of becoming viable for the present or the immediate future. The reality that any Romanian leader must confront is a continued Soviet presence.

At the same time, commitment to building a regime of national communism, the construction of a mass party organization, and the development of mechanisms for mobilizing the majority of the Romanian population have necessitated movement away from commitment to international communism and an outright pro-Soviet policy of the sort identified with the prewar and immediate postwar party leadership. More so than any other single postwar Romanian leader, Ceaușescu has consciously sought to identify the state and the party with the Romanian masses in such a way that nationalism and socialism have become synonymous and his role as leader and as sole mediator between external and internal forces unquestioned. Although there are those in Romania who could criticize the current cult of personality and the degree to which Ceaușescu has made himself and his family immediate beneficiaries of the regime's accomplishments, almost always these same people are quick to recognize that opposition to his rule could far too easily serve as a pretext for the return to more direct forms of Soviet rule.

The 1970s marked a decade of great advancement for the Ceaușescu regime – economically, through triggering accelerated industrial, commercial, and agricultural growth; politically, through the consolidation of the party's identification with ethnic Romanian culture and national aspirations; diplomatically, in the promotion of a foreign policy of multilateral relations in which it became possible to remain on favorable terms with the Soviet Union while diversifying Romanian contacts within and outside the socialist camp. The problem is, where will the country head in the 1980s? Economic autonomy has not increased greatly in the final analysis, despite recognizable advances in industrialization. Not only has Romania had to recognize its dependence on the Soviet Union as a major trading partner, but – especially in the aftermath of the Iranian revolution and its subsequent difficulties in gaining access to Middle Eastern oil (prior to the shah's overthrow Romania looked to Iran as its major foreign source) – it finds it must look to the Soviet Union for direct assistance in meeting its energy needs. Furthermore, despite strong criticism of Soviet actions in Afghanistan, it has been moving away from its role of mediator in Egyptian-Israeli relations toward closer alignment with the Arab nations along Soviet lines. While Soviet relations with Egypt remain poor and Romania's good, the overall thrust of Romanian Middle Eastern policy during 1980 was to move in a direction far closer to the Soviet position than at any time in the recent past.

Societal Constraints

Internally, there are serious problems to be dealt with that are no longer tractable as they have been for the last twenty years. The policy of identifying the PCR and the regime with ethnic Romanians and Romanian culture, as the key to building mass support, provides little consideration for the country's national minorities, especially Hungarians and gypsies. Controls over minorities remain stringent and, despite official declarations to the contrary, discrimination against these two major minorities is commonplace. If to this base is added extensive regulation of the population as a whole, the reality one confronts speaks less to effective and real mass mobilization and more to forced participation in accord with the dictates of the regime. Controls of all sorts abound in Romania as they do in the Soviet Union: required permits to move to one of the country's major cities, especially to Bucharest, are difficult if not impossible to obtain; conditions of life in rural and urban areas remain difficult; and local markets are nearly always deficient.

Increasingly there are signs within the nation's work force that continual emphasis on national development and the goal of long-term benefits for all no longer have the same appeal as in the past. The demand is for substantive improvements in the conditions of life now. Herein lies one of the ties between external and internal policy. Opposition to increased military expenditures, requested by the Soviet Union of all Warsaw Pact members in November 1978, can be linked to recognition that if more resources are to be made available for internal development and to increased salaries and social services, increases in the country's military budget must be held off. There have been signs of growing unrest and discontent in the labor force, most notably the August 1977 miners' protest against conditions of work, low salaries, and limited benefits.

Under such circumstances, with growing internal tensions and in-

creased external pressures reducing the regime's ability to act in-
dependently, the immediate prospects are continuation and tightening of
the present style of rule: Stalinism. In the Romanian context Stalinism
means reinforcement of the current leadership cult, emphasis on tight internal controls over all aspects of national life, barriers to effective
cultural exchanges among nationals and foreigners (except to permit the
careful, controlled entry of foreign academics), and extensive use of nationalistic rhetoric. This does not preclude announced reforms, such as
the call for decentralized management in accord with the Yugoslav example (as was the case in 1978); it does stress that the substance of
policy, as practiced and implemented, will change little in the years
ahead.

Socialist versus Capitalist Dependency

The reality of dependency, be it under capitalism or socialism – as
has been the case with Romania – is the absence of meaningful choice in
determining a nation's internal and external policies when it comes down
to crucial issues. To understand this reality one must distinguish between the rhetoric of nationalism in internal as well as external affairs
and the substance of policy. As Fernando Henrique Cardoso has pointed
out, using the Brazilian example, associated dependent development
under capitalism makes possible a certain amount of growth and progress, provides for a national leadership committed to a country's development, and permits limited autonomy. The substance of this argument
can be extended to the socialist bloc by using the Romanian example.
National communism, as initiated by Gheorghiu-Dej and brought to fruition under Ceaușescu, constitutes a clear case of associated dependent
development under the forms of state socialism. Just as Brazil has begun
to exhaust the possibilities of further development under the current
model and its government has had to revert to coercion to maintain the
system in 1980, so the options available to the current Romanian regime
have begun to run out.

The danger, however, is not further bloc disintegration but the
greater use of force to maintain the status quo. Where a country such as
Romania stands little chance of being able to increase its own national
autonomy under socialism along the lines, say, of Yugoslavia, the effective option becomes recourse to greater control and regulation of national life and rigidification in the regime. Almost assuredly the response
to pressure for change from within will not lead to further relaxation in
governmental controls, for that would necessitate moving beyond the
current limits of the system and thereby invite direct Soviet intervention.
Thus, it is likely that the 1980s will see an increase in internal regula-

tion and a return to closer cooperation with the Soviet Union in substantive areas, along with an attempt to maintain an image of independence from Soviet policy.

None of this will mean, however, automatic acceptance of Soviet dictates on questions of national policy; it will mean that without effective autarky there is no basis from which to build a distinctively national regime under state socialism that is different from the present model. This does not preclude radical change nor a sudden realignment of political and economic forces; it does call attention to the fact that once again when change comes to this society it is far more likely that it will proceed from the international context. This is why current trends in Poland warrant such careful study, and why Ceauşescu's statements about the unacceptability of that regime's handling of labor issues vis-à-vis Romanian internal politics and his equally strong condemnation of the prospects of Soviet intervention in Polish affairs are not contradictory in the least.

The Sino-Soviet split of the early 1960s provided a favorable environment within which the Romanian leadership could push for greater national autonomy after a decade of extensive as well as intensive Soviet influence and control over national life. But further "liberalization" under Ceauşescu is neither likely nor possible. As Romania moves into the 1980s, its eyes must remain fixed, as they have for more than three decades, on the Soviet Union. Geographical proximity and ideological compatibility preclude any other option for the present.

CONCLUSION

At the outset two themes were emphasized: Romania's status as a bridge country in the wider European context and the utility of taking the most-different-case approach in comparative politics as a way of capturing the dynamics of Romanian society. Beginning its modern history as an independent state in accord with a French institutional model and self-conscious Westernization, Romania after World War II underwent forced Sovietization and experienced a reassertion of Slavic influences over national life until ethnic Romanians assumed control of the PCR and embarked on a policy of adapting Marxist-Leninist principles to national realities. Today, both physically and psychologically, Romania remains on the fringes of Europe with one face to the East, the other to the West. Its wider significance from the standpoint of other developing states, especially those in southern Europe and Latin America, lies in its experiencing associated dependent development – first under capitalism and more recently under socialism – without having encountered an easy solution to its historic desire for political and economic independence.

Recapitulation

A very old people with a long history as a distinctive cultural entity in southeastern Europe, Romanians have found neither sovereignty nor autarky to be easily attainable. It was not until the end of the nineteenth century that a viable Romanian national state emerged in the Balkans that in some way was compatible with those people who identified themselves as ethnic Romanians. A conservative system that sought to maintain traditional class relations while pursuing Western-style modernization, it survived only as long as Great Power involvement in the region was minimized — first through the decline of the Ottoman Turkish and Austro-Hungarian empires and later with the collapse of the three imperial systems that had so long shaped the politics of this region: the Turkish Caliphate, the dual monarchy of Austro-Hungary, and tsarist Russia. The disappearance of the first of these in areas east of the Carpathians and north of the Danube was synonymous with the formation of the Old Kingdom; the second, with the acquisition of territories to the west long considered integral parts of western Europe; the third, with the removal of a cultural and political influence that supported within Romania boyars and church officials opposed to Westernization. Fear of the Russian Revolution and determination to build strong ties with the dominant European powers became the pretext for reactionary politics during the interwar years.

The outcome of World War II precluded the survival of Old Romania. With Soviet hegemony in Eastern Europe unchallenged, Romania became, as did its neighbors, a Soviet satellite. Unlike Hungary and Czechoslovakia, however, it developed its own national leadership and form of national communism without deviating from Soviet definitions of Marxist-Leninist orthodoxy. Opting for a policy of negotiated autonomy within the socialist bloc, both Gheorghiu-Dej and Ceaușescu supplied the sort of leadership that solidly identified the PCR with ethnic Romanians, the majority of the nation's population, and made possible two decades of substantial socioeconomic progress.

The Romanian model has permitted the creation of a form of associated dependent development under state socialism that has been particularly well attuned to Romania's needs as a developing nation. The initial premise was recognition of Soviet preeminence in the region and the fact that direct challenges to that hegemony would trigger immediate and direct Soviet action. Accepting that fact as indisputable for the present, Gheorghiu-Dej embarked on a policy of developing a Marxist-Leninist organization in Romania that would become solidly identified with historic aspirations: the consolidation of an independent Romanian nation-state. Under Ceauşescu this policy was brought to fruition, within the constraints that had been accepted previously: the pursuit of national interests over those of international communism, as defined by the Soviet Union, when the two came into conflict, but always without altering in any of its fundamentals the Leninist model developed and imposed in the early 1950s.

Form versus Reality

Throughout these years of rule by the PCR there has been a constant interplay between what may be called socialist ideology and socialist reality. Socialist ideology, as proclaimed by the Romanian Communist party and the state, emphasizes multilateral foreign policy promoting good relations with all friendly peoples, equality in all aspects of life, balanced planning and development under a command economy, a dynamic regime at the service of the people, ethnic Romanian leadership identified with nationalism, and the maximization of popular culture.

Socialist reality, in the sense of day-to-day living in contemporary Romania, is markedly different. In light of the state's monopoly on communications and image building, the foreign observer must be ready to distinguish between the official image of the country – created and reinforced by carefully selected visits to ideal factories, apartment complexes, stores, and the like – and the actual conditions of work, life, and shopping encountered by the average citizen. Day-to-day life is hard; working hours are long; conditions of work are constraining; public transport in the major cities is crowded and difficult to obtain during rush hours; food and commodity items are limited and in short supply. Everywhere one is conscious of his or her participation in the life of a developing country and the regime's commitment to escape from historic patterns of underdevelopment.

Within such a context there are a number of anomalies that are perhaps best explained by posing opposites. The first is secular versus religious identity. Marxist-Leninist ideology stresses the values of atheism and projects a view of society in which organized religion will gradually wither away until it disappears as a major force in Romanian life. The reality is one of great vitality among all religious groups, within which the Romanian Orthodox church enjoys a privileged position. In building a thoroughly national regime, the PCR has had to recognize the important role of Orthodoxy, historically and currently, in maintaining a strong cultural identification among ethnic Romanians.

In terms of daily living there is a constant tension between the commitment to egalitarianism and the reappearance of privilege in all aspects of life. In an economy in which so much is limited in availability and luxury items are virtually unobtainable on the local market, the struggle for goods in short supply or available only under limited conditions becomes ferocious. In such a context, the value of desired commodities bears little relationship to local currency values; instead, the effective currency becomes access – the gaining of superior position over one's competitors, whereby access to the desired item becomes realizable. Along with access comes the ability to obtain stable foreign currencies, *valută*, with which one may acquire commodities in special stores not open to the general public. Under the new state, privilege continues but the difference is that it is more readily hidden from public view, in a variety of ways – in the type of apartment made available, in the stores to which one has access, in the ability to obtain a car, in the ability to extract desired services, be they those of a skilled mechanic, excellence in health care, entry into one of the country's major academic institutions, or preferential placement in a job once one's academic studies are completed.

Within the world of formal politics the contrast is that between mass mobilization and participation, on the one hand, and elitism, on the other. The rhetoric of the regime emphasizes the importance of the mobilization of the whole society, ample participation in mass organizations identified with the Socialist Unity front in accord with one's profession or occupation, and an open, two-way planning process in which the citizenry is consulted and involved at the grass-roots level. The reality is that of a limited number of decision makers identified with the leadership of the PCR at the national, regional, and local levels. Embodying the actual decision-making powers of a limited number of individuals is the emphasis on the vesting of crucial responsibilities in the hands of a limited number of individuals through the fusion of state and party roles and the hierarchical patterns of authority whereby all essential control is maintained by those at the center and converges around the person of the first secretary and president of the republic.

This particular contrast in the world of formal politics leads to another pairing: the values of collectivism versus those of personalism. A tremendous public emphasis is placed on collective decision making, collective action, collective work in all walks of life. Carried over into the realm of public services – transport, health, urban services (water, gas, sewerage and garbage disposal), education, food and commodity distribution – the image is one of distribution to the society at large, the collectivity. Yet, against these practices must be juxtaposed the values of personalism. In official politics the cult of the leader is widespread and ever present. At every level of government it is the corresponding executive official – the *judeţ* first secretary, the town or village *primar* – who is first among equals. Within the government bureaucracy, it is likewise the office head who is the crucial official with whom one must deal. At the level of services where the public at large constitute the recipients, an elaborate set of rituals has developed for impressing one's individuality – special need, special consideration – on the bureaucrat or clerk responsible for the service. Scarce commodities or services are always kept in reserve; hence, to extract them one must have a way of impressing on the person providing the service one's individuality. While these forms of exchange vary greatly over time, during the period I was in Romania, Kent Long cigarettes were the most widely used medium of exchange for obtaining special services and commodities in short supply or of a quality above that available on the local market.

A final pairing of opposites is the contrast between the revolutionary character of the regime's Marxist-Leninist ideology and the practice of government, which is authoritarian, elitist, and conservative in character. In an environment where working-class images are continually used, the practice in government offices – where great emphasis is placed on protocol, on the proper way of doing things, on the procedures to be followed in arranging this or that program – all hark back to an administrative style of a bygone era. This aspect of bureaucratic reality, when coupled with the physical images maintained by government office buildings belonging to previous eras, gives to the present party state a distinctly bureaucratic air, one more attuned to the bureaucratic politics of authoritarian regimes – with their limited pluralism and limited participation – than the image cultivated and maintained of a mass society. The limited nature of decision making and limited access to positions and distribution centers of privilege and prestige have their foundation in large part in the institutionalization of the regime and in the form of rule exercised by the new class of party bureaucrats – in a society in which the party and the state have become one and in which there are no checks on those who have a monopoly of power.

Disjunctures of this sort abound in contemporary Romania. The very nature of the regime and the long history of this culture as one that has survived despite tremendous odds make it a society difficult to penetrate and understand. It is a country shot through with enigmas regarding its operations and processes and patterns of politics, society, and economics. Yet, in the midst of the impersonality that has come to characterize the extensiveness of the modern Romanian state, it is the continued cult of close personal relations and contacts and intimacy that gives to this people and this society a vitality and fascination that is worthy of admiration.

NOTES

1. Romanian–U.S. Economic Council, U.S. Section (Jay A. Burgess, author), *Romanian-U.S. Joint Ventures: Background for Implementation* (Washington, D.C.: Chamber of Commerce of the United States, 1974), pp. 1–2, 5–7. These page numbers, as well as information contained in the preceding paragraph, document this accord.

2. Nicolae Ceauşescu's report to the Tenth PCR Congress as quoted in National Council for Science and Technology, *Science and Technology in Romania* (Bucharest: NCST, 1977), p. 13.

3. *Science and Technology in Romania*, p. 17.

4. *Science and Technology in Romania*, p. 23.

5. The relevant legislation is Decree No. 275/1973 and Law No. 91/1973, as cited in *Science and Technology in Romania*, p. 23.

6. The phrase "Leninist dependency" is adapted from a recent study by Kenneth Jowitt entitled *The Leninist Response to National Dependency*, Research Series No. 37 (Berkeley: Institute of International Studies, University of California, 1978). It can be compared and contrasted with the concept of capitalist dependency as developed by Fernando Henrique Cardoso and Enzo Faletto, *Dependencia y desarrollo en América Latina* [Dependency and development in Latin America] (Mexico: Siglo XXI Editores, 1979) and James A. Caporaso, "Dependence, Dependency, and Power in the Global System: A Structural and Behavioral Analysis," *International Organization* 32:1 (Winter, 1978).

Annotated
Suggested Readings

PREFACE

Tagliavini, Carlo. *Le origini delle lingue neo-latine: introduzione alla filologia romanza* (Bologna: Casa Editrice Prof. Ricardo Patron, 1959).
> For those interested in language as the structure through which culture is communicated, this source is indispensable. It offers an excellent introduction to modern Romanian and its ties with the other Romance languages. It is not, however, to my knowledge available in an English language translation.

CHAPTER 1. NATIONALISM AND THE FORMATION
OF AN INDEPENDENT ROMANIAN STATE

Braudel, Fernand. *The Mediterranean and the Mediterranean World in the Age of Philip II*, Vols. 1 and 2 (New York: Harper and Row, 1973).
> Throughout this extensive study of the Mediterranean world in the era of Philip II of Spain, Braudel stresses that the interplay between the fundamental unity of the Mediterranean world (an area in which he includes the Balkan peninsula) and its very great diversity gives this region its distinctive character.

Fischer-Galati, Stephen. *The Socialist Republic of Romania* (Baltimore: The Johns Hopkins Press, 1969).
> Although dated, this short study still constitutes the best single overview of the government and politics of Romania under communism. His basic characterization of the regime remains as valid today as it was at the time of publication.

Hoffman, George W. *Regional Development Strategy in Southeastern Europe: A Comparative Analysis of Albania, Bulgaria, Greece, Romania, and Yugoslavia.* (New York: Praeger Publishers, 1972).

See his discussion of Romania, both the country profile and the overview of its development strategies at various points in the book, for a useful summary of contemporary Romania in its broader geographic, historical, and socioeconomic setting.

Jowitt, Kenneth, ed. *Social Change in Romania, 1860-1940: A Debate on Development in a European Nation,* Research Series No. 36 (Berkeley: Institute of International Studies, University of California, 1978).

This collection of essays on prewar Romania provides an excellent introduction to those aspects of Old Romania most relevant to understanding contemporary Romania.

Matley, Ian. M. *Romania: A Profile* (New York: Praeger Publishers, 1970).

As an introduction to modern Romania, this book's greatest strength is its summary of the historical development of Romanian culture and the formation of an independent Romanian nation-state.

CHAPTER 2. THE DESTRUCTION OF OLD ROMANIA AND THE CONSTRUCTION OF A NEW SOCIALIST ORDER

Barbu, Z. "Rumania," in S. J. Wolf, ed. *European Fascism* (New York: Vintage Books, Random House, 1969), pp. 146-166.

This is an excellent summary of fascism in Romania. Read in the context of the introduction by S. J. Wolf, its place within the broader European context becomes clearer.

Elsberry, Terence. *Marie of Romania: The Intimate Life of a Twentieth Century Queen* (New York: St. Martin's Press, 1972).

A sympathetic biography of King Ferdinand's British wife, who adopted Romania as her homeland after her marriage. Through her eyes one can develop a good understanding for Romanian society and politics as seen from the vantage point of the old elite.

Ionescu, Ghiţa. *Communism in Romania, 1944-1962* (London: Oxford University Press, 1964).

This book by a Romanian emigré documents in detail historically what was entailed in implanting a Marxist-Leninist regime in Romania.

Janos, Andrew C. "Modernization and Decay in Historical Perspective: The Case of Romania," in Kenneth Jowitt, ed. *Social Change in Romania, 1860-1940: A Debate on Development in a European Nation* (see Chapter 1 listings for complete citation), pp. 72-116.

Janos' chapter summarizes extremely well the nature of politics and society in prewar Romania.

Nagy-Talavera, Nicholas M. *The Green Shirts and Others: A History of Fascism in Hungary and Rumania* (Stanford, Calif.: Hoover Institution Press, 1970).

For those interested in the Iron Guard Movement, this book contains a detailed discussion of fascism in Romania and its relationship with the related right-wing movement in Hungary during the period before World War II.

Roberts, Henry L. *Romania: Political Problems of an Agrarian State* (New Haven: Yale University Press, 1951).

> Considered by many to be the most useful single study in English of Romania between the wars and of the immediate post–World War II changes, up through the installation of the Groza government.

Weber, Eugen. "Romania," in Hans Rogger and Eugen Weber, eds. *The European Right: A Historical Profile* (Berkeley: University of California Press, 1965), pp. 501–573.

> Given the significance of the right as a political force before World War II, this particular essay offers the reader insight into the groups and structures that the Romanian Communist party was determined to destroy after World War II. It summarizes succinctly what Nagy-Talavera describes in detail.

CHAPTER 3. THE REKINDLING OF NATIONALISM UNDER SOCIALISM

Fischer-Galati, Stephen A. *The New Romania: From People's Republic to Socialist Republic* (Cambridge: MIT Press, 1967).

> This book constitutes, in my opinion, the most complete discussion in English of the evolution of Communist party rule in Romania and the operation of the regime under Gheorghiu-Dej and the transition to rule by Ceauşescu.

Floyd, David. *Rumania: Russia's Dissident Ally.* (New York: Praeger Publishers, 1965).

> This particular book, although a general treatment of Romania as a whole, is helpful today for the insight it gives into the resurgence of nationalism in Romania during the rule of Gheorghiu-Dej.

Jowitt, Kenneth. *Revolutionary Breakthrough and National Development: The Case of Romania, 1944–1965* (Berkeley: University of California Press, 1971).

> While this is a difficult book for the neophyte, it warrants mentioning in two regards: its development of the concept "revolutionary breakthrough" and its analysis of Marxist-Leninist thought as it pertains to the construction of a socialist society in Romania.

Jowitt, Kenneth. "An Organizational Approach to the Study of Political Culture in Marxist-Leninist Systems," *American Political Science Review* 68:3 (September 1974), pp. 1171–1191.

> This article gives an insightful overview of the building of a socialist society, incorporating general political culture perceptions and a case study of Romanian experience.

CHAPTER 4. DEVELOPMENT: FOR WHOM AND FOR WHAT?

Gilberg, Trond. *Modernization in Romania since World War II* (New York:

Praeger Publishers, 1975).

   More than any other source, this book attempts to summarize the Romanian experience with modernization (or development) policies under
   socialism. It offers the reader detailed information on the overall thrust and
   the results of Ceauşescu's policy of multilateral development.

Montias, John M. *Economic Development in Communist Romania* (Cambridge, MIT
Press, 1967).

   Published by MIT Press as a complement to Fischer-Galati's *The New
   Rumania,* it offers a knowledgeable overview of the development of the
   Romanian economy, probably the most complete and readable such treat-
   ment in English.

Nelson, Daniel. "Local Politics in Romania," unpublished doctoral dissertation,
Johns Hopkins University, 1975.

   A very readable and easy-to-understand overview of local-level politics in
   contemporary Romania.

Turnock, David. *An Economic Geography of Romania* (London: Bell, 1974).

   This detailed analysis of the Romanian economy, in the context of its
   geographic setting, offers background data concerning the overall development of the Romanian economy during the 1960s and the early 1970s. Its
   primary contribution is as a source more recent than the above-mentioned
   work by Montias.

CHAPTER 5. EXTERNAL RELATIONS:
LENINIST DEPENDENCY AND THE OUTSIDE WORLD

Cardoso, Fernando Henrique. "Associated-Dependent Development: Theoretical
and Practical Implications," in Alfred Stepan, ed. *Authoritarian Brazil: Origins,
Policies, and Future* (New Haven: Yale University Press, 1973), pp. 149–157.

   Recognizing that the literature on capitalist dependency is extensive, this
   chapter gives the reader an understanding of the point of view of one of the
   leading proponents of capitalist dependency – Cardoso – in a way that can
   be compared and contrasted with Romanian experience.

Farlow, Robert L. "Romania: The Politics of Autonomy," *Current History* 74 (April
1978), pp. 168–171 ff.

   This article summarizes the general thrust of Romanian foreign policy effectively, accurately, and provocatively.

Jowitt, Kenneth. *The Leninist Response to National Dependency,* Research Series
No. 37 (Berkeley: Institute of International Affairs, University of California,
1978).

   This study is really the first to raise the issue of dependency relationships
   within the socialist bloc in a way that is comparable with the major
   capitalist dependency literature. Despite the utility of this concept for
   Romania, however, this is primarily an essay about the general conditions
   of underdevelopment to which Leninist theory responds – with examples

drawn from the Romanian case. It contains little, if any, discussion of what happens once the Leninist model is installed.

Smith, Hedrick. *The Russians* (New York: Time-Life Books, 1976).

This perceptive analysis of Russian society by a former *New York Times* Moscow correspondent is quite useful in understanding the dynamics of the Soviet model as it operates in Romania. While there are obvious major cultural differences, the structure of society and its functioning in Romania is much the same as it is in Russia because of the political structure imposed on Romania three decades ago.

Index

DATE DUE

GAYLORD PRINTED IN U.S.A.